"By the time you finish the introduction, you will know beyond a shadow of a doubt that Kyle Lake is someone you want to listen to. By the time you finish the first chapter, you will know that this book is straightforward, honest, transparent, and lacking all of the silly church expressions that have become intolerable to thinking people. As you continue to read you will find new ideas. You will find classic ideas expressed in new ways. And you will find that prayer is still one of the big surprises of the spiritual journey."

—**GORDON ATKINSON,** pastor, Covenant Baptist Church, San Antonio, Texas, and author of Reallivepreacher.com

"*(Re)Understanding Prayer* is a book that offers a fresh perspective for anyone who has ever felt like they're personal prayer life is less than stellar. I laughed out loud as Kyle poked holes in some of my own personal prayer expectations. This is a book that really takes the pressure off praying and will help you focus on what really counts."

—**ROB SPERTI,** regional leader for 24-7 Prayer

"The last thing we need is another book on prayer that is full of platitudes and euphemisms. Thank God that Kyle Lake has the ability to look at Christian prayer for what it really is: the maddening, beautiful, confounding, inept attempts of human beings to communicate with our Creator. This book is a gem!"

—**TONY JONES,** national coordinator for Emergent-U.S. and author of *The Sacred Way*

[RE]UNDERSTANDING PRAYER

(RE)UNDERSTANDING PRAYER

A FRESH APPROACH TO CONVERSATION WITH GOD

KYLE LAKE

[RELEVANTBOOKS]

Published by Relevant Books
A division of Relevant Media Group, Inc.

www.relevantbooks.com
www.relevantmediagroup.com

Design by Relevant Solutions
Cover design by Joshua Smith, Jeremy Kennedy
Interior design by Jeremy Kennedy

Library of Congress Control Number: 2005902186
International Standard Book Number: 0-9763642-6-3

For information or bulk orders:
RELEVANT MEDIA GROUP, INC.
100 SOUTH LAKE DESTINY DR. STE. 200
ORLANDO, FL 32810
407-660-1411

06 07 08 09 9 8 7 6 5 4 3 2

Printed in the United States of America

TO UBC IN WACO, TEXAS

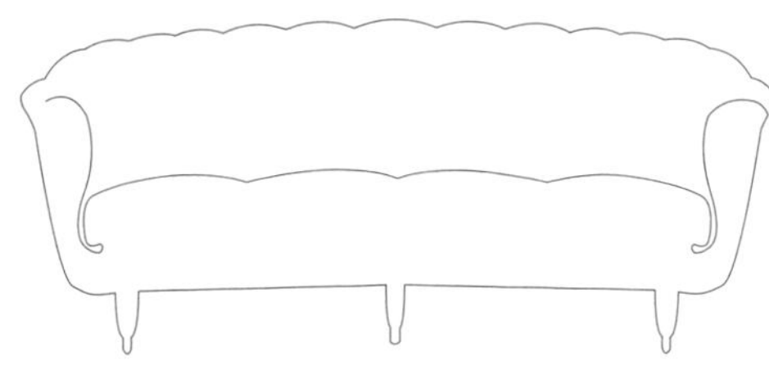

CONTENTS

FOREWORD BY DAN KIMBALL

Prayer, as most of us are well aware, is one of the most foundational aspects of being a disciple of Jesus. We all know Jesus prayed and told His disciples to pray. We all have read in Paul's letters in the New Testament that we are supposed to pray. In our churches, there is probably an annual teaching series on prayer, where we sit and listen to three to five weeks of sermons about how we are supposed to pray. We may have a dear grandmother or hear the legend of someone elderly in our church who is one of those mysterious "prayer warriors." In Christian circles we hear little phrases about people having a "prayer closet." Or hear someone say that the "Lord spoke to me this morning in prayer during my quiet time." We feel guilty and wonder why we aren't getting messages like that when we pray.

Knowing how important prayer is, we get motivated to pray. We buy the tapes of the pastor's last sermon series on prayer and relisten to it. We hear in his sermons how he is one of these early risers who gets up at 5:00 a.m. and prays for an hour. So, we set our alarm, and for three or four days we actually get up. We may not pray quite an hour, but we are trying, and we feel that God is happy with us. But the fourth day comes along, and we sleep in. By the fifth day, we have given up. It is back to normal. Guilt. I am not a good disciple. Jesus got up early in the morning and prayed; I can't even wake up, and now I'm late and can't even make it on time to class or work, and I haven't even prayed. More guilt.

So we hear about a book that gives four steps on how to pray. The book lays out a simple plan. Four specific steps to praying each day. It even has a companion journal to buy to write out your prayers. You read the book. You start using the journal. You ignore the pink little floral pattern that edges the prayer journal. You even doodle a face to hide one of the flowers. You do this for a week. You are amazed at the prolific language you are writing out. Using New Testament words you never ever say in real life. But by the second week, something feels wrong. You are wondering if what you are writing in your journal is more about sounding spiritual; you are more worried about how they sound than what you really are experiencing. You get sick of looking at the little flowers on the prayer journal you bought. You don't feel like going through the four steps anymore. You stuff the prayer journal into a drawer. Guilt. You are defeated again.

Fast-forward to you at a church retreat. The speaker sends you off for an hour to go have a "quiet time" with God. In the beauty of the camp you are staying at, you find yourself praying like you haven't in a long time. You have nice wonderful mornings, hanging out by the lake and praying as you flip through pages of the Bible. This is it! You feel like you are getting a rhythm going. You are finally praying like you want to. But the day you get back from the retreat, you have to go back to school or work. You can't just sit by the lake and ponder life and pray. You are late again, rushing out to the car to get to where you are going. More guilt. Should you even try to pray anymore?

Kyle is about to show you that perhaps the way we struggle and think about prayer isn't really God's guilt. Instead it is something that we have heaped on ourselves out of false expectations of what prayer really is. When we look at the Bible with a fresh perspective, maybe prayer is something that is not quite as hard as we think.

As you read Kyle's words in this book, maybe you will find yourself seeing your own reflection in many of the stories he shares. Maybe you will be enabled to admit some of the things that you have thought about or felt but couldn't quite put into words. Or if you did, you would get some questionable stares from the pastor who just gave a sermon on how you are supposed to pray, and this doesn't quite fit.

We must pray. Prayer is essential to our life, like breathing. Without it, we die. That is why this book is so refreshing and so needed. It helps you breathe again. It takes some of the tightening off your chest, and it lets you just stop and breathe ... and pray. You don't think a lot when you are breathing. It is natural. It just happens. When you are nervous or in a panic, you may need to slow down and catch your breath. Just like prayer.

I did a quick search on Amazon.com, and there are more than nineteen thousand books listed that have the word "prayer" in the title. However, this book that you are about to read is not a typical book about prayer by any means. In fact, it is more different than any other book I have read about prayer. You are about to read quite possibly the most honest, raw look at prayer. But I bet as you read it—instead of guilt, instead of yet another formula, instead of a new method—Kyle's words will encourage you just to slow down and breathe ... and pray.

—Dan Kimball
Author of *The Emerging Church*
www.vintagefaith.com

AUTHOR'S NOTE

I've never owned a book on prayer. I don't know why. It may be the same reason I have difficulty reading instruction manuals before fumbling through technological devices, except that with prayer you don't have to return anything once you've screwed it up. You just live in the aftermath of smashed seven-step programs, ploys, and platitudes that have been strewn across the floor in a fit of anger. I wonder if this is how many people backpedal their way out of prayer. Perhaps it's not for a lack of long-winded religious instruction. It's just that the manual didn't hold an ounce of earthly meaning. And that's why I wrote this, with people in mind who are somewhat disenchanted with prayer—who probably don't have a book on prayer on the shelf and for very good reason. The pages that follow are intended to describe what prayer would look like if pulled out of subculture Christianity. Along the way, I made sure to address issues that have always been cloudy for me as well—like how do you distinguish God's voice from your own, what do you make of supernatural phenomena, and how do you understand prayers that seemingly go unanswered? Essentially, I wrote a prayer book for non-prayer-book readers. My hope, then, is that this book wouldn't make you more religious, but more alive to God.

ACKNOWLEDGMENTS

Jen, Avery, Sutton, and Jude. Dave, Toni, Ben, and Jamie. Mom and Dad, Jody and Steph, Jona and April, Kristi and JD, Rick and Janice, Scott and Crystal.

Jason Mitchell, Craig Nash, Blair and Jordan Browning. Thanks also to Holly Jones and Faith Korpi for allowing the use of their emails. Also to Matt Bates, who prompted the idea behind chapter 4, prayer as social dance. Thanks also to Harris Bechtol, Valerie Targhetta, Matt Singleton, and Lacy Urbantke.

Several authors and resources have been influential—from the likes of J.B. Phillips, N.T. Wright, Larry Crabb, Rob Bell, Tony Jones, Todd Hunter, Phyllis Tickle, and Brian McLaren. Dallas Willard's *Hearing God* was especially instrumental in the latter chapters on understanding the supernatural, discerning God's voice from your own, and deciphering answered from unanswered prayer. Willard has proven to be an excellent resource, especially on such weighty subjects.

Jill and the kind folks at Common Grounds, home of the Cowboy Coffee.

Cara Davis, Tia Stauffer, Jeff Jackson, and Cameron Strang—along with the rest of the great staff at Relevant.

INTRODUCTION

It seems backward to begin by saying that I struggle with prayer—being a pastor and all.

"You mean you struggle understanding prayer OR you struggle at times understanding the point of prayer OR you struggle actually praying?"

Yes.

Within other professions I could be sued for malpractice. And yet I would contend that my prayer diploma was never legit in the first place. It was a mail-order thing I found on the Internet for fifty bucks, but the Old English font makes it look quite credible on the wall.

I was practically birthed in the church, and, aside from a little off-time I took in college, I've been there ever since. On the low end I'd ballpark some 243,360 hours have been logged within a church setting over the course of my life. So with that much pew time, you could just about say my diploma came from the acclaimed Juilliard School in New York City.

Apparently, I've been doing theater for several years now. I'm like John Cusack sitting comfortably with more than forty films under my belt, a proven track record, and a file full of scripts. I'm loaded with lines from my past, and at any moment I can break into character ...

LLOYD DOBLER

"I gave her my heart, and she gave me a pen."

(John Cusack) *Say Anything ...* (1989)[1]

MARTY BLANK

[Practicing in a mirror before his high school reunion]

"Hi. I'm, uh, I'm a pet psychiatrist. I sell couch insurance. Mm-hmm, and I—and I test-market positive thinking. I lead a weekend men's group; we specialize in ritual killings. Yeah, you look great! God, yeah! Hi, how are you? Hi, how are you? Hi, I'm Martin Blank, you remember me? I'm not married, I don't have any kids, and I'd blow your head off if someone paid me enough."

(John Cusack) *Grosse Pointe Blank* (1997)[2]

CRAIG SCHWARTZ

"Nobody's looking for a puppeteer in today's wintry economic climate."

(John Cusack) *Being John Malkovich* (1999)[3]

ROB GORDON

"My desert island, all-time, top-five most memorable breakups, in chronological order, are as follows: Alison Ashmore, Penny

Hardwick, Jackie Alden, Charlie Nicholson, and Sarah Kendrew. Those were the ones that really hurt. Can you see your name on that list, Laura? Maybe you'd sneak into the top ten. But there's just no room for you in the top five, sorry. Those places are reserved for the kind of humiliation and heartbreak you're just not capable of delivering."
(John Cusack) *High Fidelity* (2000)[4]

The only difference between Cusack and myself—my stage is prayer. God is the casting director. And I've been auditioning for the past twenty years ...

KYLE LAKE
[with an English accent]
"O most Holy One of Cherubim and Seraphim, wouldst Thou lend Thine ear. Thine wonders shine forth in a dazzling array of splendor. Just as Thou hast answered our prayers with the miraculous rain, hear us now and moisten the dryness of our hearts with Thine dew of divine life."
(played by me) *Real Life* (1985)

KYLE LAKE
"Yo, G-dog. I wanna send some mad props in yo dy-rection and ask that You be with me and my homies. We're gonna be doin' some drive-by witnessin' at the mall tonight. Help us get all up 'n their grill with the Word so the heathen 'll be turnin' from their evil ways."
(played by me) *Real Life II: Jesus, My Homeboy* (1991)

KYLE LAKE

"Dear Lord, be with us now in these moments because we know, Lord, that where two or three are gathered in Your name, there You are in their midst, Lord. Just help me to let go and let God. May I love the sinner but hate the sin. Help me to get right so I don't get left. I mean, I've got to stand for something or I'll fall for anything. I know You love me just as I am, but too much to leave me there. Bring a fresh move of Your Spirit so all of us believers can stand in the gap as You raise up a new generation. Yes, Lord, Your pain is definitely my gain. In His name. Amen."
(played by me) *Real Life III: Murder by Cliché* (1995)

Like Cusack, more scripts are on file than I can count, and, sadly enough, I could channel any particular prayer at the drop of a hat. Place me in any church setting, and with perfect fluency I can become a local. Drop eight Scripture references and six clichés in one prayer? Easy. Pray the name of Jesus against assorted demons and any other nearby terrestrial beings? Done. Use Shakespearean language with Sean Connery inflection? No problem.

But remove all the clichés and the familiar lines I've voiced for several years, and I'll sit there without a word to speak for hours on end. Sad but true. I've virtually been raised in the church, and familiarity has become my greatest enemy. Like an actor differentiating himself from his character, I've had an identity crisis—one that sounds similar to what author and psychologist

Larry Crabb experienced during his own revolution within the therapeutic world.

In an interview Crabb was asked the question, "How do you heal a soul?" And in mocking response he retorted that it doesn't have anything to do with listening skills—something he refuses to teach. "Repeat what the other person says ... Lean forward ... Eye contact ... I just despise that! Then I'm just doing skills toward you, instead of being with you."[5]

In similar fashion, those who've spent any length of time within a church setting have picked up on the skills, methods, and techniques of prayer—the correct physical posture that will yield direct connection with the Divine, the most ardent emotion that will certainly get His attention, a proficient vocabulary of spiritual words and phrases assured of moving His hand. But Eugene Peterson, author of The Message, would say that those of us who have taught or learned the trade are simply "peddling techniques."

"The world is full of so-called prayer warriors who are prayer-ignorant. They're full of formulas and programs and advice, peddling techniques for getting what you want from God. Don't fall for that nonsense. This is your Father you are dealing with, and he knows better than you what you need" (Matt. 6:7-8, MSG).

Imagine that. Could it really be possible that some of the very people we've always thought to be "prayer warriors" are truly "prayer ignorant"? Could it be that we've entered a day and age when the fluent, polished prayer warriors shouldn't be mimicked? And in its place, the truest prayer warriors might actually be stumblers and fumblers? They've shed contrivances and devices for simply getting what they want from God or hearing what they want to hear. And in exchange, they've demanded meaning from their words. They've abandoned cliché, drama, and formulas for something with less zing but more substance—struggle, thoughtfulness, and an eye for a holistic faith. In the pages that follow I want to renegotiate this age-old topic—prayer—in an effort to move beyond immaturity, legalism, and a compartmentalized faith. If our conversations with God should be indicative of anything, they should point us toward becoming authentic, mature, whole-life followers of Jesus. Certainly, then, that is my aim.

I've got to also acknowledge the arrogance in a book on prayer whose very title is re- anything ... re-understanding, re-creating, re-inventing. Anyone could reasonably question, "How can you possibly act as though you are providing a 'new' perspective on an aspect of life that's been in existence, well, since the beginning of time? How arrogant and foolish could you possibly be?" Very true. And, honestly, all I can assure you is that this perspective has definitely been (re-) for a number of people in my own community of faith. In a sense, I write this for them with the hope that they are indicative of many, many more. Many of the folks in my church were raised in a variety of church settings—Baptist, Catholic, Nondenominational, Methodist, Presbyterian, Lutheran—but found themselves at a place, like me, where their prayer lives were floundering.

Strangely enough, their staggering toward prayer has been because they are people of profound truth. In other words, they haven't struggled because they've become less interested in God or less desirous of following Jesus, but the opposite. They continue experiencing God in various ways, but the only framework for prayer that they've known has been loaded with vacant banter and trite expressions. This collided with the core of who they are. To be people of integrity, many of them felt they had two options: one, pray to God with the same familiar rehearsed lines and old clichés; or two, don't pray at all. From one angle, you could say their "lack" of a prayer life has been noble. In this book, I will show that all they needed was for someone to come along and brick the roads they were already traveling. And, in the process, we will rediscover a means of interacting with God that is truthful, life-giving, and holistic.

1
CHAPTER
NUKED

On March 17, 2003, President Bush issued a forty-eight-hour ultimatum for Saddam Hussein and his sons to leave Iraq. Military conflict was imminent. I watched the president's address to the nation from my living room in Hewitt, Texas, just twenty-five miles from Bush's Crawford Ranch, and I remember the feeling of apprehension that war was, in fact, near. The entire nation knew we were inches away.

The next morning I was awakened at 3:15 by a distinct alarm sounding off outside of my house. What could that be? It definitely didn't sound like a car alarm. Assuming it would soon be silenced, I quickly went back to sleep. Thirty minutes later it was still sounding, so I got out of bed and went into my boys' room that looks out the front of our house. I opened the blinds to examine the street left and right to try to decipher from where this alarm was sounding. No luck. It definitely wasn't coming from this side of the house. It was coming from the back. So I walked into the living room, approached our back door, opened the blinds, and examined the area directly behind our house.

A thick fog covered the area from the ground up, making it even more difficult to locate, so I opened the door and stepped out about ten feet onto our back porch. (Our house is one of many cookie-cutter *Pleasantville* models, so even distinguishing my house from the others in my own backyard requires precision.) Within seconds I knew the alarm was definitely coming from this direction, but I still couldn't find its exact location. I climbed up onto the patio table centered on our back porch to peer out over the fences and figure out what was going on. And as soon as my feet were firmly planted on the table, I picked up my head, and THERE—IT—WAS! ... An orange-tinted, mushroom-shaped cloud billowing up from the ground *in the direction of Crawford!*

NO WAY!

Saddam Hussein has one-upped Bush and nuked the Crawford Ranch just eighteen hours before the ultimatum expired! Of course! Those crafty Iraqis!

Wait.

What is the blast radius of a nuclear bomb? Nuh-uh. It's got to be more than twenty miles. I've gotta load Jen and the kids in the car and drive east as quickly as possible!

> (*running back into the house and into the bedroom*) "Jen, wake up! Come here, quick! The Crawford Ranch has been nuked!"
> "What?"
> "The Crawford Ranch! You know, the ultimatum!"
> (*drowsy*) "Huh?"
> (*pulling her outside, onto the back porch, and pointing*) "Look!"

After clearing the sleep from her eyes, she squinted off into the distance. And I will never forget her response. I've harbored heavy bitterness ever since.

In the most condescending tone, she turned to me and scowled back.

> "That's the Hewitt water tower."
> "Ohhhhhhhhhhhhhh."

A red light sits atop the water tower and, at night, continually blinks to warn planes or helicopters in the area. During a fog as thick as what we had that night, the light's redness blurs to a haze, casting an orange hue over the entire tower. I swear you would've taken one look at that thing at 3:15 in the morning—just hours before the ultimatum expired—and thought, "Yes. That is definitely a nuclear explosion. There are no two ways about it."

But rather than feeling as though I had been duped, I was actually relieved. I mean, a week without marital communication I can deal with when compared to the split-second disintegration of my flesh and bones. Somehow the thought of total annihilation is a wee bit more difficult to embrace.

Fortunately and unfortunately, I've had this experience a number of times. Not mistaken nuclear explosions, but experiences in life where what I perceived to be real was in fact not real at all. Some of these experiences have been spiritual in nature because they pertain to how I've understood God, or rather misunderstood God; how I've understood Scripture, or rather misunderstood Scripture; how I've understood the nature of prayer, or rather misunderstood the nature of prayer. When God, Scripture, and prayer create 98 percent of your worldview, you can imagine how jarring it can feel to have someone or something come along and tilt the axis on which your world has spun for more than thirty years. At times the jolt is so overwhelming that I choose not to accept it and simply continue along my merry way. It may be truth, but truth is not welcome when it comes at such a high price. The hollow cavity it creates in the pit of my stomach cannot be worth whatever awaits on the other side, or so I tell myself. And that works for a while ...

THE UNKNOWN

There are those times, however, when I actually wade out into the unknown and explore the possibility that things are not as they seem. Not out of some extraordinary display of courage on my part but due to some very tangible reasons. Believe me, I'm not the fearless type. I have friends—Brody, Sloan, and Jed—who habitually search out the next cliff to jump, a steeper ascent to climb, a higher class of river navigability to kayak. They are adrenaline junkies. They're the Tasmanian Devils of extreme sports. I, on the other hand, have vowed not to live life on the edge. I am Winnie the Pooh.

So my wading out into the unknown, my pushing of boundaries, my exploring of terrain is hardly admirable. Again, it's simply due to some very tangible reasons. Reasons that are quite logical and at times intermingled with a spot of intuition.

Reason #1: God in a Box

My experience of life outgrew my understanding of God. Pure and simple. At some point, I was overcome by the realization that the God I was raised worshiping could not handle the complexities of real life. He was perfectly fit to deal with lollipops, candy canes, and sugarplums, but avalanches, wildfires, and tsunamis He was not. Literally and metaphorically.

What's odd about this realization is not its ridiculous nature but my response to this realization. The next few years I shifted into a defensive posture. I became protective of God, like an older brother watching out for his diminutive little sister who couldn't hold her weight on the school playground. And this posture eventually seemed odd to me. Why did God need defending? Who was I really protecting?

Reason #2: Vacant Mentors

For more than ten years, I had my own personal pope a guy I thought to be the quintessential perfection of spirituality. But somewhere along the way, my model of faith—the person I patterned my life after—became someone I did not want to be. I examined the trajectory of my life and didn't like where it was headed. For instance, my personal pope regularly went public with the messages he'd heard from God. Only a few times was this information announced as if through a megaphone; most of the time his announcements were far more subtle. Eventually, I began to realize that the people who spoke most often about God telling them this or God telling them that were also (ironically) arrogant, self-seeking, and artificially humble.

Now this, I thought, was odd. If God is going to speak to humans, won't He always point them in the direction of being fuller, deeper, more loving, more responsible followers of Jesus? And if that's the case, why do those who claim to have experienced God's personal communication leave their encounters with a sense of superiority? It's ironic. Shouldn't an active prayer life breed a person whose resemblance mirrors Jesus? It would make much more sense to have a dormant prayer life and therefore choose Satan as a comrade, but that was not the case. So I began re-evaluating all of the terms, parameters, and byproducts having to do with prayer and was reminded that someone once said, "Perhaps we should give up our good Christian lives and follow Christ." So maybe, just maybe, some forms of prayer promote "good Christian lives" while other forms of prayer promote the actual following of Christ. Is this possible?

Reason #3: Christianity's Eastern Roots

As I grew older, I began to realize that the word "prayer"—as it has been taught and defined to me—could not fully describe all that was included in my communication with God. I know, I know, this sounds odd. In fact, I regret to say that after spending some 243,360 hours within the walls of various churches to date, I began approaching prayer with the mindset of what counts—and what doesn't count. This is somewhat disgusting. It's almost like me emailing my wife an entire conversation from work one afternoon. Then, once I get home, I'd walk through the door and say, "We don't really have to talk tonight, right? I mean, you did get the email I sent this afternoon ... and that counts, right?" My wife may only be five foot two, but I tell you, she works out. Somehow I think I missed the point. Especially after a shot to the gut, I now KNOW I missed the point.

Saving me from such legalism and compartmentalization, a good friend walked me through the differences between a Western mind (which I, an American, function with) and an Eastern mind (which Jesus, a Hebrew, probably functioned with). Without this crucial conversation, I'd probably still be approaching my prayer life with bar graphs, pie charts, tables, and diagrams, plotting data and quantities along a certain set of axes—and, in the process, entirely missing the point.

Thankfully, I somehow became more Eastern in my approach to God and faith even while living in central Texas—a feat that rivals the feeding of the five thousand or the raising of Lazarus from the dead. When I say "Eastern," I'm not saying that I've started confining my dress to sandals and a turban and begun hitting the tanning bed four times a week. Please. I'm as Caucasian as you can get. Instead, I'm saying that somehow, someway an entirely different orientation toward God and, in particular, the presence of God has become my own. This Eastern mindset, which I believe will provide much of the fuel for our conversation, will be elaborated on in chapter 8.

In the meantime, the next six chapters will be spent elaborating on reasons #1 and #2. I believe the need for some healthy level of deconstruction is paramount to any learning/growth process. That is, some amount of time should be spent unloading baggage, albeit a healthy unloading. No matter what we are trying to discover or rediscover—whether it be something as deep as our own identity or simply a craft like crochet—a natural part of that learning process involves distinguishing what you should do as opposed to what you shouldn't do, or who you should be as opposed to who you shouldn't be. In other words, the unloading aspect of the learning process is natural and vital; however, I've realized that tons of people get off on the unloading part. There's something satisfying about being the renegade who lives life for the sole purpose of shooting the wheels off other people's methods, interests, practices, and ideologies. That's why I intentionally use the word "healthy" ...

My end goal isn't destruction but construction. How lame would it be to spend 90 percent of my time demolishing and only 10 percent of my time rebuilding? Heck, what about 70/30? Still lame. Because there's no risk or identity involved there. The critic's chair is and has always been the safest seat in the house because the critic defines himself by what he is not. It's an entirely different way to live when you actually step out and explore, affirm, create, re-create, invent, and reinvent. Much of this book will be spent doing just that.

2
CHAPTER
MIXED MESSAGES

We communicate so many things in so many different ways. Our lives are constantly communicating. Sure, we primarily use words to express our thoughts, intentions, and who we are, but words can be so misleading. Come to think of it, is there any form of communication that's true through and through? Is there any form of communication that can't possibly send its audience in the wrong direction? Email, instant messenger, and chat rooms aren't exactly the answer. In fact, you could argue that the Internet actually encourages people to form false personas and impressions that hardly represent who they really are and what they really think. It's almost impossible to find some form of communication that sends fully honest messages.

But I'm convinced people underestimate the deceptive power of the hair. Let's get real—no matter who you are or where you live, your hair communicates. Sure, you could explain the level of recession that's left you with a small tract of land, but the question is, what have you done with what's left? (Without turning to hair replacement, I'm trying as hard as possible to mask my own.) Or you could say that you only spend a few bucks every six months on hair products, and therefore you couldn't care less about what your hair is communicating. But even that lack of interest is communicating a message. Something is going on there, albeit the message is, "I give squat about what my hair communicates." Still, don't be misled. That is a message.

For the past several years, I have donned some variation of the unkempt hair. Shaggy unkempt. Chaotic unkempt. Spiky unkempt. Faux-hawk unkempt. For some time now, my hair has tried to communicate, "Hey, I woke up about eight minutes ago, threw on some clothes, and got here as fast as I possibly could. This is the way I live—very laissez faire because that's who I am. I couldn't care less what people think. I'm edgy, reckless, and disorganized. There's absolutely no forethought to what I will do next. I'm unconstrained and frequently put my own life at risk." When, in fact, this couldn't be further from the truth. In reality, I have three kids. And I admit I stood in front of the mirror this morning arranging the hair for at least three minutes. Actual thought processes took shape to form some sort of conclusion about what I would wear. Actual thought processes! Why? Because I completely care what other people think. I'm fairly organized, intentional, and currently vying for legal ownership to "my space" at a local coffee shop where I practically live. I'm a creature of habit. But the hair is trying its darnedest to communicate otherwise.

It's amazing how many different directions we can send people who are searching for our true identity. For some, it's an art form. Within the first thirty seconds of conversation, they could be sent from The Shire to Mordor and back again—a sad journey for people simply interested in friendship.

Prayer, on the other hand, is difficult to fake. Well, personal, one-on-one, alone prayer is difficult to fake. Eliminate the audience, become a fly on the wall, and you'll notice the thing that's created there in that space between the individual and God says it all. Want to find out what someone thinks of God? Listen to the way they pray and how they pray it. There, in those words and posture, is everything—how they view and approach God, life, faith, relationships, vocation, meaning, the past, the present, the future. And more importantly, what role does God play in the grand scheme of things?

Is God an autocrat, a puppet master, or a perfectionist? Is God a magician, a machine operator, or a vending machine? Or is God something else entirely? Can God affect change in a given situation (work environment, illness, relationship), or have all events been stapled in time for us to simply respond to? Is God generally silent, or is God quite vocal? Is life a giant jigsaw puzzle that God originally created, then disassembled, and then created us for the purpose of putting it back together? Or is life truly a journey of leaving The Shire, and if so, what role does God play?

In the end, you could have misunderstandings about a number of things that, unbeknownst to you, radically shape the way you relate with God. It's the same sort of phenomenon that takes place when parents are trying to choose a name for their first child. If the parents are going to be democratic about the choosing, then they could very well be in for a looooong and sometimes violent road.

The wife suggests a possibility, "What do you think of Taylor?" Even in her presentation, she voices the name as if she's uncovered a bag full of diamonds. In her head, trumpets begin sounding the very second "Taylor" is announced, because she's only been considering this name for, oh say, the past twelve years.

Poor husband. Sitting duck.

In a matter of seconds, the wife finds "Taylor" violently thrown to the ground. She's shell-shocked and leaves the room dejected, and the husband finds himself handed a pillow and stale blanket to use while sleeping on the couch for the next two weeks.

Or turn the table. The husband suggests a possibility, one that he's been considering for, oh say, the past twelve minutes. It's a name he saw on the side of a building on the way home from work that day—only to find this name violently thrown to the floor in a matter of seconds. And he, too, storms off as if he's held this name dear to his heart since junior high. Unbeknownst to either of them, molten rock has been hiding below the surface. Both have had a wealth of experiences with people named Taylor and Jonathan, Alissa and Harris ...

It's an interesting phenomenon. If a name is suggested of a specific person that you or your spouse knew in high school but *did not like*, you'll not let that name fly if your life depends on it. When a name is mentioned, specific associations immediately surface that are attached to that name. It's just not humanly possible to separate the alphabetic symbols—T-A-Y-L-O-R—from the time this particular person in your tenth grade chemistry class (who went by the name Taylor) created a rumor that you paid high dollar to sit in the fifth row at the Backstreet Boys concert. Taylor never fessed up to having said such a thing even though four people pointed in that direction, and the two of you were never the same.

A few months ago, I had a friend in Houston tell me he and his wife were having a little boy. Brimming with pride, they said, "And we're going to name him Philip." I'm sure somewhere in a distant land trumpets were sounding, but not near me. Naturally, I responded with lies. "That's so great! What a great name."—all the while thinking—"Are you kidding me? I knew a Philip once, and you *do not* want to name him that! Unless, of course, you want him to consume large amounts of cocaine, but hey, that's your business. Philip it is!"

And this phenomenon is not confined to expectant parents; it's found in almost every area of life ... One individual grows up in an abusive home where the father is an angry alcoholic—physically, verbally, and emotionally abusive. Later in life, this person walks into church for the first time in years, and they hear God addressed as Father. Immediately, their stomach knots up, and they start looking for the exit sign.

Or string together the alphabetic symbols—P-R-A-Y-E-R—and immediately corpse-like sentiments are evoked because all that's ever been known has been lifeless, rote, legalistic ritual. Or what immediately comes to mind is the time in college when that church guy wanted to "pray over" your diabetes and told you if you had enough faith and confessed enough sin, you could no longer be a diabetic. Or the time you heard a conference speaker say, "God was talking to me the other day and ..." You, however, left feeling miserable because you've never experienced that level of open communication with God, and there's only one reason ... it must be due to your lack of spirituality. Or maybe the word "prayer" doesn't evoke sentiments of monotone, lifeless duty, but hyped, emotional, super-spiritual drama just as lifeless with more words and heavier breathing.

If we are going to push toward a real, whole-life, interactive relationship with God, we must be willing to cut ties with misunderstandings—perhaps misunderstandings we picked up along the way or even misunderstandings we were explicitly taught.

3
CHAPTER
THE MESSAGE-A-MINUTE VIEW

According to the message-a-minute view[1], you and I are part of the Secret Service. We're CIA—which is pretty cool when you think about it. I've always wanted to be part of the CIA or FBI, and seeing how I have a knack for locating nuclear explosions, I'm well on my way.

There exists on this planet a breed of ultimate, highly mature, super-Christians. These individuals are our end goal. They provide us with something to shoot for, something to aspire toward. Each and every one of them has a special Miracle Ear hearing aid molded to the edge of their ear canal. I'm sure they were given these earpieces by their Bible study teachers or church small group leaders after memorizing one hundred verses or reciting the Lord's Prayer in Greek. The Secret Service has these too, only theirs connect to the pipeline of restricted, highly confidential government ops—"operations" for those of you not familiar with our language. When the Secret Service agents are out in public with the rest of the commoners, they will at times need to apply more pressure to the earpiece with the use of their index finger to block out the surrounding noise.

In other words, the highest possible goal for us to attain is for God to send us messages every minute of every day. This is what takes place among those who are most in tune with God.

> "Put on this shirt, not that shirt."
> *"Yes, God."*
> "Don't eat Raisin Bran today. Go with Banana Nut Crunch."
> *"Yes, God."*
> "Go to the coffee house before the drug store, not after."
> *"Yes, God."*
> "Turn left. Now make a right at the second stop sign. All right, stop right here ..."
> *"Yes, God."*

My sophomore year in college, one of my buddies told me how he had miraculously scored an 88 on an exam. Sam had forgotten to study for a test, walked into class, and was surprised to hear he had an exam that day. So he prayed. And wouldn't you know it? God walked him through the exam informing him how to answer every step of the way! Spiritual Miracle Ear came through loud and strong ... B, B, A, D, C, B, C, A.

At the time, I was amazed and envious all at once. "Wow, God is so incredible! I wish I had that level of relationship with God. That's hardcore!" But if I heard this load of crap today, I would call him on it. (Not to mention, how did God get an 88 and not a 100?) Wouldn't a more mature follower of Christ actually study? Isn't studying and being aware of the exam schedule a sign of responsibility? So wouldn't God always be pushing us toward becoming more mature, responsible people? Or is He really wanting us to develop into reckless, irresponsible people who give no thought or intention to the paths we choose?

At the heart of prayer, we must be aware of God's end goal for our lives—that we are continually becoming fully present, fully alive learners of Christ. Certainly, then, the healthiest sort of prayer should help get us there. God couldn't have actually created us to be robots without brains, personalities, gifts, and abilities, could He? And if that's not who we are, does it affect our prayer lives in the least? Wouldn't the message-a-minute view actually *impede* our growth? In his book *Hearing God*, Dallas Willard says, "In close personal relationships conformity to another's wishes is not desirable, be it ever so perfect, if it is mindless or purchased at the expense of freedom and the destruction of personality."[2]

Hiding behind this view lie several destructive versions of God—God as puppet master, dictator, machine operator, or taskmaster. Any of these descriptions fit because they all reduce the human person to a slave at the end of a whip or a mechanical device that performs by the assistance of a lever. Oddly enough, though many Christians strive to find more interaction with God, some truly want prayer to be nothing more than dictation. And dictation has nothing to do with encouraging the developmental process of maturity and responsibility. It only perpetuates immaturity and irresponsibility.

We as Christians have been led to believe that when we make decisions without the guidance of a burning bush or a well-placed billboard, we are acting *apart* from God. In fact, many Christians have been taught that when we make decisions (rather than God dictating them to us), then we've just stepped off into a world utterly void of God. We've somehow been taught that our living, breathing, moving, deciding, going-in, and going-out lives are mutually exclusive from our spiritual, fasting, praying, Bible-reading, "God told me to" lives. Again, I'll elaborate on this much more in chapter 8, but suffice it to say that the apostle Paul didn't seem to receive dictation from God on every step of his journey throughout Athens and Corinth, yet he fully felt as though God was present in every inch of space surrounding his body (Acts 17:28).

It's become difficult for us to imagine God wanting *us* to make decisions, both big and small. And why would God want such a thing? Because God's end goal is that we become mature learners of Christ (Matt. 28:19-20). It's in the process of making decisions that we experience maturity and take ownership of our lives. In fact, the term "learner" lies at the heart of the Greek word for "disciple," *mathetes*.

In no way should it be assumed that these decisions are made in isolation or outside of conversation with God. I'm assuming the opposite is already taking place. We should already be living in the context of a faith community where we are in continual conversation with God and consistently reading the Scriptures. Again, in later chapters I'll take aim at erasing the box we've drawn around our experience of God.

At the heart of prayer is a dynamic, interactive relationship involving God and human, not God and slave or God and lawn mower. Perhaps at a deeper level, we would do well to absorb the full essence of Genesis 1:31, "God saw all that he had made, and it was *very good*" (emphasis mine). To be human—and not slave or lawn mower—is good. I'm convinced that many of our destructive tendencies are rooted here, for either we lose our way by thinking too poorly of ourselves or too highly.

It is good to be human—and not God. There is only One.

As well, it is *good* to be human—and not robot.

4
CHAPTER
THE FOXTROT

Step, step, kick, turn. Step, step, kick, turn. Step, step, kick, turn. Step, uh-oh, step-kick, turn, step-kick, uh-oh, uh-oh, kick-step, kick, kick. #@&★%!

We are pubescent eighth-graders learning the art and etiquette of formal dance for the very first time. I remember this class vividly. Every Thursday night, the second—no, nanosecond—I walked in the door to the class, I made a mad dash to the side of the room where the rest of my buddies were huddling. Initially, the guys congregated on one side of the room while the girls stood on the other. The level of hormonal change and energy in that single room could probably be bottled, compressed, and used to launch a space shuttle.

A number of dances were explained by an elegant and articulate lady in her early sixties who had the spunk of a sixteen-year-old. It was as if she lived for the Waltz, Rumba, Tango, and Foxtrot. She'd begin the class with a brief description of the dance for the night. I'm convinced her explanation was so enmeshed with the dance in her head that it was spoken with rhythm, melody, crescendos, and decrescendos ...

> The Waltz is a smoooooothprogressivedance characterized by loooongflooooowingmovements, continuous turns, riSE and FAAaall. Graceful and elegant, Waltz dancers gliiiiiiide around the floor almost effortlessly. *(stretching her left arm as far as it could possibly stretch)* Some forms of the Waltz are punctuated with lavish open movements, (*while arcing her right arm over her head like an umbrella, she'd begin turning beneath it and spinning way too many times*) underarm turns, and solo spins.

All right already! We get your point!

Then, my heart would begin pulsing in rapid succession as she'd pair the guys and girls randomly. *Please, please, put me with Molly! Put me with Molly!* But she never did. She always seemed to have it in for me. I didn't even know the lady, so I couldn't figure out what I ever did for her to have developed such a vendetta. The old hag. Then she'd step out into the middle of the dance floor and motion one of the moves for the night, like the Left Box Turn (or, as some may say, The Box Step).

> The actual amount of turn that one can take over the course of these six steps is optional—anywhere between a one-eighth and three-quarters turn may be applied, depending on your skill level. Now class ... CLASS! Listen up! This is IMPORTANT! With any more than a three-quarters turn, the Left Box Turn becomes an entirely different step known as the Left Cross Turn. You all probably saw this step in the movie *Top Hat* with Fred Astaire and Ginger Rogers. ... *Yes, sure we did* ... The Left Cross Turn can be seen in the Viennese Waltz.

I always loved this. I loved all the times she'd use insider dance language in her explanations as if we knew exactly what she was talking about. Perhaps there were times when she found greater satisfaction in dropping words beyond our reach than ensuring we were actually learning the steps.

> With any less than a three-quarters turn, the Box becomes a *spot movement* used for turning corners, realigning oneself to set up for a particular pattern, or confining oneself to a small area of the dance floor. If you students become advanced in the Left Cross Turn, you will actually use the Left Box Turn to travel down the line of dance, but this must be done with precision. The man must begin facing a *diagonal center alignment* and take the Left Box Turn with exactly a three-quarters turn to end facing diagonal center. This is often done in combination with the Right Box Turn, resulting in a sequence of consecutive turns which enable the dancers to travel around the line of dance.

Social Dance was a staple in the developmental process of an eighth-grader in Tyler, Texas. It was a cultural norm, an assumed rite for many of my friends—guys and girls. Our parents, though, probably had us enrolled in Social Dance for reasons more subconscious than conscious due to the fact that today I'm not too proficient in the Foxtrot. When approaching my female counterpart on the dance floor, I learned the appropriate address. "Madam, may I have this dance?" Then, if I receive a positive response, I escort her to an open area of the floor. I place my right hand, slightly cupped, on her waist. Placement here is crucial for an eighth-grade boy. Then, with left hand held moderately high at shoulder level and elbow out at a forty-five-degree angle, I hold her hand with a certain level of firmness between my thumb and index finger, and we Left Box Turn the night away.

I think from our parents' perspective, 95 percent of this class had nothing to do with dance and everything to do with etiquette and respect, but I could be wrong. Maybe our parents were countercultural protesters trying to preventively combat all the grinding that would be going on in high school. Maybe they held a joint meeting, and someone with a prophetic voice stood up from within the crowd and said, "If we train up our children in the ways of the Cha-Cha, they will not turn from it in later years." And after several Amens, we were enrolled.

Either way, etiquette, respect, and structure are important. At an early age, my prayer Waltz was ACTS, an acronym designed as railroad tracks for those learning how to pray. **A**doration-**C**onfession-**T**hanksgiving-**S**upplication.

ad·o·ra·tion n.
1. The act of worship.

2. Profound love or regard.

con·fes·sion n.
1. The act or process of confessing.

2. Something confessed, especially disclosure of one's sins to a priest for absolution.

3. A written or oral statement acknowledging guilt, made by one who has been accused or charged with an offense.

4. An avowal of belief in the doctrines of a particular faith; a creed.

5. A church or group of worshipers adhering to a specific creed.

thanks·giv·ing n.
1. An act of giving thanks; an expression of gratitude, especially to God: a hymn of thanksgiving.

2. **Thanksgiving** Thanksgiving Day.

sup·pli·cate v.
1. To ask for humbly or earnestly, as by praying.

2. To make a humble entreaty to; beseech.

3. To make a humble, earnest petition; beg.[1]

I don't know the originators of ACTS, but my guess is that it was developed by people who saw the need for prayer to be something more than self-absorbed ad-libbing. A kind of prayer-on-training-wheels to push me beyond a self-centered monologue. What a necessity. In one sense, prayer has the potential to create an even greater level of self-absorption, therefore defeating my pursuit of Christ. With a tool like ACTS, though, prayer can be more. It can actually be others-oriented.

And yet, I don't know that a thing like ACTS or other teaching devices were ever meant to be the end goal, although it's become that for some. I've heard it said that "imitation is the first form of learning," and if that's the case, ACTS can be a great tool. However, there must be a time in all relationships where we begin to stand on our own two feet. There should be a time when we're no longer fixated on the placement of our steps ... was it step, step, kick? Or was it step, kick, turn? Or step, step, kick, turn?

For some, though, this won't register because prayer is actually defined by etiquette and formality. It is about precision and polished perfection. Words with a Victorian flare. "O most Holy One of Cherubim and Seraphim, wouldst Thou lend Thine ear. Thine wonders shine forth in a dazzling array of splendor. Just as Thou hast answered our prayers with the miraculous rain, hear us now and moisten the dryness of our hearts with Thine dew of divine life." All fine and good when British scholar N.T. Wright is the one praying, but when this is not your normal mode of communication, it won't be long before you're diagnosed with Multiple Personality Disorder.

In the process of debunking Prayer as Social Dance, the fundamental question to ask is: Is God primarily interested in technique?

If He is, then we should do our best to watch the placement of our steps. We should pay careful attention to the rhythm and cadence of our words. Perhaps our prayers should become replicas of our pastor's and Bible study leader's prayers if God is primarily interested in technique.

I've listened to some people pray and thought that, surely, they're about to break into song. It's like they're human airplanes slowly achieving liftoff. Starting slow ... picking up speed ... more speed ... faster ... Faster ... FASTER ... LIFTOFF!

Now this is odd. It's not just odd, it's freakish. Why would God create you with a distinct personality, then turn around and require you to pray apart from it? Hidden beneath your skin is a mosaic of mental, emotional, behavioral, and physical qualities, plus gifts, talents, interests, and abilities peculiar only to you. If those things have actually been created by God, wouldn't it be sacrilegious to intentionally create a space to communicate with God and then fill that space with an entirely different person than yourself? It would be contemptuous and disrespecting, not just to God but also to you.

Certainly, the Creator is interested in your own personality where He is continually turning you inside out, not giving you more steps and charades to learn. Right? The Scriptures say, "This is your Father you are dealing with, and he knows better than you what you need. With a God like this loving you, you can pray very simply" (Matt. 6:8-9, MSG). In Psalm 139 David says to God, "I'm an open book to you; even from a distance, you know what I'm thinking ... You know me inside and out ... You know exactly how I was made, bit by bit, how I was sculpted from nothing into something. Like an open book, you watched me grow from conception to birth; all the stages of my life were spread out before you" (Ps. 139:2, 15-16, MSG).

5
CHAPTER
D-A-DOUBLE D-Y-M-A-C

It was 1992. How did I—a purely Caucasian, blond-haired kid three years removed from a full set of braces—get to a place where I actually prayed to God, "Yo, G-love. What up. Straight chillin' here in T-town. Wanna kick it with You today 24/7. I can't be frontin'. Gotta come correct and live J-style today, Lord. Help me pop those demons with tha Word. And if I step outta line today, get up in my grill with tha truth. I'm out. Peace."

Let me back up and retrace my steps. The year 1992 was an interesting time on the music front. Eighties hair metal was a sinking ship. Grunge music was a fledgling newborn developing into its own style. Hip-hop was still on the outside of the pop music industry looking in, thanks in large part to the violent image of Gangster Rap. And then, along came Kris Kross, the coolest twelve-year-old kids you'd ever seen.

How could you ever forget the D-A-double D-Y-M-A-C? Classic tracks that made you jump, jump. The unforgettable hits "Warm It Up" and "I Missed the Bus" had suburban preteens bobbing their heads and left their parents without a complaint.

Since the album lacked profanity, Kris Kross' worst possible influence on adolescents at the time involved wearing baggy jeans and baseball jerseys backward.

Now enter: young, obnoxious youth pastor (me). Twenty years old. First job tending/guarding/herding a couple of hundred sheep ages twelve to eighteen in a large suburban church. Entirely too much responsibility at the time. And at my disposal, a cultural phenomenon known as Kris Kross just waiting to be exploited.

In a moment of remarkable inspiration, I felt the CD cover screaming out at me: "Look, Kyle. Kris Kross. Change the 'K' to a 'C' on the second word, and you've got the name of your summer Wednesday night gathering at church! It's brilliant! Creative, innovative, relevant. The students will love it. You can even encourage them to wear their clothes backward! How riotous would that be?"

So in April and May I began promoting our summer Wednesday nights with posters and mail-outs that had the Kris Kross logo on it saying,

COME AND KICK IT WITH US THIS SUMMER AT KRIS-CROSS!

WHY?

BECAUSE WE'RE TOTALLY CROSSED-OUT!

(CLOTHES WORN BACKWARD STRONGLY ENCOURAGED)

Unbelievably cutting-edge. The first Wednesday night of the summer, we had a room full of 150 youth coming in the door with their pants and shirts on backward. Half of them wore baseball caps that were turned backward or to the side. Bass was pumping. I'm telling you, they loved it. When they walked in the door, our theme song of the summer was playing, a song by E-Roc called "Down with the G.O.D." ... because we were ... and that was a good thing. Being "down," that is. Maybe "down" was the '90s equivalent of the '80s word "bad."

Here were all these kids from suburbia "down with the G.O.D." We even developed our own lingo that I'm confident didn't originate in the neighborhoods where these kids were raised. Language like, "Yo, me and Jesus, we're like home boyz" (if written, always with a "z"). "Yo, J.C., He got my back, yo. We like Blood Brothaz" (or, words ending with an "az"). And when we'd say these things with our clothes and caps on backward, we'd even created our own sign that represented the honest-to-God truth that we were, in fact, gangsters for Jesus. We'd cross our middle two fingers—the bird and the one next to the pinkie—then cock the wrist toward the ground. At times our sign was held over the heart when saying our farewells. (Naturally, we'd never be caught dead saying the word "farewell." Usually, something more along the lines of "peace" or "peace out.") All of these things proved indeed we were a bunch of misplaced suburban kids who were really from the hood.

And the students loved it. Every Wednesday night they couldn't wait to show up with their backward apparel and lingo as we pumped "Down with the G.O.D." through the speakers. Even the parents loved it because their kids couldn't wait to get to church. This was youth ministry on the edge, I'm telling you. Innovation and creativity at their best.

Anyone who's spent any length of time working with a room full of thirteen- and fourteen-year-olds realizes you have to contextualize your message to some degree. I mean, how many fourteen-year-olds really relate to and connect with their grandparents who are fifty and sixty years older than they? So if a thirteen-year-old can't relate to a sixty-five-year-old, what are the chances they're going to relate to a Man who walked the earth two thousand years ago? And yet this is precisely the problem.

The majority of people at our church in Waco have parents who were born in the '40s and '50s. If the parents grew up in a church setting, then chances are they were adorned with their best attire every Sunday morning. While there, they were on their best behavior. When God was mentioned, He was described in a deep booming voice that made you shiver in your boots. When He was prayed to, a holy reverence and flowery language were used. And if you had a question about what God looked and sounded like, you could probably look at your awe-inspiring pastor to get your best guesstimate. All in all, the '30s, '40s, and '50s suggested that there is a qualitative difference between who God is and who we are.

Now, fast-forward to the '60s, '70s, and '80s when many people in our church were born ... within these years came the "Jesus movement," and, to a certain extent, the notion of God became romanticized. The phrase "quiet time" popped up during these years, and the spiritual emphasis shifted to having a "personal relationship" with God. To say "I am going to have my quiet time alone with God" is like saying "I am meeting with God for a romantic rendezvous." The church was no longer emphasized as the resting place for God, but just one of many places where I can experience God. The key thought: God is with me—just like a best friend—wherever I go. All in all, the '60s, '70s, and '80s suggested that God is, in truth, not a remote, distant God but that God is my God.

My point is not that either one of these eras was better than the other. The point is that there is a significant aspect of the '30s, '40s, and '50s that should be relearned. When dealing with junior high and some high school students, you have to contextualize. There is the constant effort to make God relevant, to take God into their world, to make God easily understood, to make God fit. In the process, it somehow becomes easy for us to see Christ and ourselves as sort of enmeshed as one. I can think of several times in my past when I said with absolute certainty that God was leading me to do this or that, but in retrospect I'd have to question the validity of at least half of them.

I'm learning the reality of the passage in Isaiah 55 that our parents' generation seemed to understand so well ... that God is not always like me. His ways are not always my ways. His thoughts are not always my thoughts. His values are not always my values. And, despite my best intentions, His goals are not always my goals. This perspective allows us to approach God with humility, recapture that holy reverence, hold loosely to our version of who He is, and—in the inevitable days ahead when our ways, thoughts, values, and goals conflict with His—realize we are the ones who do the changing.

THE TRANSITION

Fortunately, there is a natural transition that takes place among most people somewhere between the ages of fifteen and thirty. Or I should say at least one transition (sometimes more). In childhood and even into early adolescence, our understanding of reality and our primary form of faith are borrowed. That is, our worldview has not only been shaped by but literally adopted from a parent, uncle, aunt, grandparent, teacher, pastor—some absolute authority outside of us.

Who is God? "My mom says ..."

Should you hit other people? "My dad says ..."
Should you use the word "hate"? "My parents say ..."

Outside influences create a world of black and white/good and evil where we follow the rules without question. But somewhere along the way, our borrowed faith becomes more personalized. It's almost as if our parents' worldview is monogrammed on our sleeves with our very own initials. We begin to embody and experience day-to-day events that reinforce our parents' worldview. Our favorite Spiderman watch is stolen, and in the process we learn that stealing is, in fact, not right. We are lied to about how many pushups Jimmy can do, and in the process we learn that lying is, in fact, not right—just like our parents, teachers, and/or pastors told us. Borrowed faith becomes personalized faith, and this personalized faith stays in tact for many, many years.

That is, until we learn the world is not as simplistic as we once thought. It can't be oversimplified into black and white/good and evil. And here we encounter one of the more significant transitions of our entire lives. Through personal experiences and further learning, we are shocked into discovering that our comfortable way of being in the world no longer works. We're ravaged by a messy divorce, an ugly church split, the betrayal of a friend. For some of us, we are not given the opportunity to smoothly transition into a natural rite of passage. We're shoved into it with brute force that jerks our heads back. Our previous modes of thinking, our former versions of reality are thrown to the ground.

Other times, though, this transition is more subtle. It doesn't signal its arrival with a bullhorn. Instead, it is a slow, persistent chipping away at your understanding of reality—but a definite dying nonetheless. Maybe it's realizing your coworker who has little to no church involvement lives a more selfless, Christlike life of integrity than many of your friends who've spent the better part of their lives inside the church. Previously, because of his low church attendance, he was so easily branded "evil," but now the brand doesn't seem to fit. Through this experience with your coworker, some of the stories in the Bible take on new meaning—stories of supposed "outsiders" who actually did a better job of incarnating God than the "insiders" ... the stories of Ruth, Rahab, Uriah, the Good Samaritan, Cornelius—and the walls begin to shift in the house you've constructed for God. (Or I should say, the house we've constructed for God.)

One of the dangers of denominationalism is that you can be prone to think God exists as the Party Leader of your own point of view. And if you're not aware, there are just a few points of view out there: Christian Disciples of Christ, Church of Christ, Church of God, Covenant Church, Evangelical Covenant Church, Evangelical Free Church, Foursquare Gospel Church, Full Gospel Church, Lutherans, Lutherans of the ELCA, Lutherans of the Lutheran Missouri Synod, Mennonite Brethren, Messianic Church, Methodist Church, Methodist Free Church, United Methodist Church, the Nazarenes, the Nondenominational Church, the Nondenominational Bible Church, the Nondenominational Community Church, Presbyterian, Presbyterian Church USA, Presbyterian Orthodox, and, last but not least, the Baptists—American Baptists, Fundamental Baptists, Fundamental Independent Baptists, Southern Baptists, North American Baptists, Missionary Baptists, Primitive Baptists, Free-Will Baptists, Reformed Baptists (based on the First London Confession of 1689), Sovereign Grace Baptists (based on the First London Confession of 1646), General Baptists, Landmark Missionary Baptists, and the Old Time Baptists.

J.B. Phillips says, "If all these churches give the outsider the impression that God works almost exclusively through the machinery they have erected, and what is worse, damns all other machinery which does not bear their label, then they cannot be surprised if the outsider finds their version of God cramped and inadequate and refuses to 'join their union.'"[1]

Phillips goes on to say that if these churches that make the boldest and most exclusive claims about God also produced the finest Christian character and influence, then the outsider could perhaps forgive the exclusive claims. But that's not always what the outsider finds.

Slowly but surely, the grip we've held on our miniature versions of God begins to loosen. More of life is experienced that suggests God might be a little more than the Party Leader of our own particular views.

Other experiences continue to loosen our grip—experiences where we are reminded that God is much, much more than we ever imagined ... It's January, and you're perched atop a snow-covered mountain in Colorado all bundled up in four layers of clothes, standing on seventy-inch skis or a sixty-inch snowboard. Before heading down the slope, you pan 360 degrees and realize you are surrounded on all sides by mountains even greater than the one you're standing on, and the closest ones to you are a good twenty miles away. The snow is coming down in the most beautiful of ways. It's like nothing else, for when it falls, it doesn't yap and scream to signal its arrival. It falls without making a peep.

While standing there, you catch a panoramic view of your surroundings, and suddenly your perspective—your entire outlook on life—is brought into view. It's like your vision has been corrected for a few brief moments. You suddenly feel as though you could be swallowed whole. You're an obsolete peon who might possibly blow away at any second, and your own egocentric universe comes unraveled.

For me, the falling of snow rivals just about any spiritual experience I've ever had. I live in a part of Texas where we encounter snow about twice every twelve years. So falling snow speaks of peaceful serenity. But did you know that when snowflakes fall on the surface of water, they create a monstrous racket for water animals with a keener sense of hearing?

> Noisy snowflakes pose problems for electronic "ears" by blurring sensitive sonar readings. A team of researchers from four universities, including Johns Hopkins, produced these findings about snowflake sounds by analyzing recordings made underwater during winter storms ... The researchers concluded that as a snowflake falls onto a body of water, it deposits a tiny amount of air just beneath the surface. Before the bubble reaches the surface and pops, it sends out a piercing sound. If you submerge a pocket of air trapped in a snowflake, that pocket of air cannot just sit there ... The bubble has to adjust its volume, and it will do so by oscillating. And when it oscillates, it emits noise ... This screeching sound, ranging from fifty to two hundred kilohertz, is too high-pitched to be heard by human ears, which generally pick up nothing higher than twenty kilohertz. But the snowflake noise can be annoying to porpoises and other aquatic animals that can detect the higher frequencies. Falling snow can add thirty decibels to underwater noise levels.[2]

For you and I, the slow, steady downfall of our pinhole worldview is still a painful death below the surface even if we were never blindsided by a Mack truck. To eventually realize over time that the "voice of God" you heard on July 6, 2005, (that landed you in your present location) might not have actually been the voice of God is shooting the decibel level underwater way, way up. These realizations may not have struck out of nowhere with violent force, but they are real nonetheless.

The eventual discovery that your relationship with the Divine didn't appear out of thin air but is rooted in and connected to history's long and winding four-thousand-year-old road has diminished your feelings of originality. That the most original thought, question, or idea you've ever had about God has already been posed by hundreds of thousands of people throughout time has deepened your sense of humanness.

Or maybe it's eventually learning that the Bible has a bit more complexity than *Charlotte's Web*. You find out the apostle Paul quoted *pagan* philosophers Epimenides and Aratus in Acts 17, and weeks later you subtly begin to realize that this has now become your Scripture. "How could Paul have been so well versed in the pagan literature of his day? And, more importantly, how could pagan literature have found its way into our sacred text?" Not only has this left you reconsidering your approach to Scripture but also to life. Where exactly does God exist? How is God experienced? Previously, He was so easily compartmentalized.

Whether it's atop the mountain or sitting next to your coworker or learning the context of Scripture, whether it's over months or within seconds—a transition has occurred. Movement from one stage to the next has happened. Previously, you were trapped in your own narrative, but now you have confronted enough in life to realize that your "one right way" does not always provide satisfactory answers. And you are comfortable with paradox ... a sacred God poking His head in a filthy world. Supposedly good people doing evil things, and supposedly evil people doing beautiful things.

Logic, rationality, and science are always valued, but you've come to believe that some things cannot be explained. Rather than feeling threatened by these paradoxes, you find them comforting and awe-inspiring. Arrogance has been traded in for humility as life is lived less judgmentally.

Do not be mistaken—there is a specific way of life to embrace of which Jesus is the center. Only now, you are defined by what you are rather than what you're not. Previously, you identified with a select subgroup of people who validated your own thoughts and ideas so much that you had become an elitist critic. God was always on your side. Everything had been figured out, and no one could tell you otherwise. Anne Lamott put it this way, "You can safely assume that you've created God in your own image when it turns out that God hates all the same people you do."[3]

Now, though, you're not so sure.

Here marks one of the more significant departures of our lives. Left behind is cool, fun, hip god—Jesus-is-my-homeboy sort of god. Tame god. Convenient god. En vogue god. Makes-complete-sense god. Now, we have experienced enough of life to know that God is immeasurably bigger than our minds can hold. Left behind is the sort of god who must always fit into our world, the god who must always be relevant and contextualized, the god who must always be easily understood.

In fact, it no longer feels right to refer to Jesus as "my homeboy." Drops of fear have been absorbed into the soil of our lives. Not the sort of fear that leaves us immobilized. The sort of fear that makes us rethink the placement of our steps. No doubt, a different sort of God has been planted.

The remarkable aspect of this transition is that you and I are beginning to embrace God not just for what He does or does not do in our lives, but for who He is. Previously, God was embraced only insofar as He fit into our world. God was embraced because He was cool and fun and hip, and He spoke my language and lived in my world and was, in a sense, tame and understandable. But no longer. No more tame god. No more hip god. Or even my god. Just God. Holy, awe-inspiring, overwhelming God.

The prophet Isaiah put it this way,

> Seek the Lord while He may be found; Call upon Him while He is near; Let the wicked forsake his way and the unrighteous man his thoughts; and let them return to the Lord, and He will have compassion on him, and to our God, for He will abundantly pardon. "For My thoughts are not your thoughts, Nor are your ways My ways," says the Lord. "For as the heavens are higher than the earth, so are My ways higher than your ways and My thoughts than your thoughts." (Isa. 55:6-9, NAS)

A very different sort of prayer that does not hinge on whether God is understandable, en vogue, or safe goes like this:

> God, I hold fast to You right now for who You are, knowing full well that at this very moment You are not like me and I am not like You. Right now, my thoughts are not Your thoughts, my ways are not entirely Your ways, my values are not entirely Your values. But, God, I still cling to You, and I approach my future amid this inevitable conflict of interests between Your ways and Your thoughts and my ways and my thoughts. And when Your ways and Your thoughts conflict with mine, I will strive to be the one who changes.

6
CHAPTER
PRAYER AS DRAMA

FADE IN:

EXT. PROVIDENCE, RHODE ISLAND—WINTER MORNING

A PRETTY YOUNG WOMAN is standing on the street corner waiting for a bus. She's carrying books and looking very collegiate.

A black stretch LIMOUSINE with darkened windows drives past, SLAMS ON ITS BRAKES, and backs up.

The Young Woman stares at her reflection in the windows, wondering what this is all about.

Finally, the REAR PASSENGER WINDOW zips

down, revealing LLOYD CHRISTMAS, age thirty. He's a pleasant-enough-looking guy, but a little shaggy. He's wearing a dark suit.

LLOYD
Excuse me, can you tell me how to get to the medical school? I'm supposed to be giving a lecture in twenty minutes, and my driver's a bit lost.

YOUNG WOMAN
(heavy European accent)
Go straight aheads and makes a left over za bridge.

Lloyd checks out her body.

LLOYD
I couldn't help noticing the accent. You from Jersey?

YOUNG WOMAN
(unimpressed)
Austria.

LLOYD
Austria? You're kidding.
(mock-Australian accent)
Well, g'day, mate. What do you say we get together later and throw a few shrimp on the barbie?

The Young Woman turns her back to him and walks away.[1]

SCRIPTS

I think half of my known existence has been lived within a movie theater. I love film, and I know how it affects me when I watch an actor absorb his script. Not just the text, not just the words on the page, but an entire physical and emotional character that can suck the breath out of my lungs with a single blink. In those moments I completely forget who they are in the real world. I forget who they're married to, who they're dating, or why they just named their newborn Apple, Maddox, or Seven.

I also know how it affects me when I'm sitting there with smuggled Red Hots in hand watching an actor who might as well be reading cue cards. It's as if someone told him he was hosting *Saturday Night Live* but for the big screen. In those moments when I feel practically ripped off, like I could have done a better job than ________, I say things like "That was so scripted!" Or "He might as well have been reading from his script!" Of course, when I use this word, I'm referring to the actual text of a movie or play—a script.

However, over the past several years, this term has been borrowed by some outside of the cinematic industry. Those in the therapeutic profession have adopted the term "script" to refer to specific patterns of behavior that tend to cycle through family histories from one generation to the next ... things like depression, domestic violence, alcoholism, and suicide. Or they could be how you handle conflict, how you approach and spend money, how you relate to members of the opposite sex, what you do with your anger. These scripts may be unwritten, but they are very real and very influential. And yet they're nothing new.

In the Genesis story, take Abraham, for example. At one point, Abraham's personal safety was threatened. God had called Abraham to leave Ur and go to Canaan. When there was a famine in

Canaan, Abraham decided to go to Egypt to survive the difficult circumstances. "As he drew near to Egypt, he said to his wife, Sarai, 'Look. We both know that you're a beautiful woman. When the Egyptians see you they're going to say, 'Aha! That's his wife!' and kill me. But they'll let you live. Do me a favor: tell them you're my sister. Because of you, they'll welcome me and let me live'" (Gen. 12:11-13, MSG).

Notice Abraham's strategy of self-preservation. He was willing to sacrifice his wife's safety and honor for his own survival. In that panicky moment of fearing for his life, he ignored what God had promised him—that he and his wife would produce a great nation (Gen. 12:2). And he didn't seem to care what happened to his wife. Believing that Sarai was Abraham's unmarried sister, Pharaoh had her taken to the palace to be one of his wives. If not for God's intervention, the truth would not have come out, and the story would have ended tragically.

Years later, after Abraham's son Isaac had married Rebekah, there was another famine. Isaac went to the land of the Philistines. There he repeated what his father had done (Gen. 26:1-11). Fearing for his life, he lied that Rebekah was his sister. Later, when the Philistine king found out the truth, he confronted Isaac, who confessed that he had been afraid of losing his life. As in Abraham's case, this happened just after God had promised Isaac that his descendents would be as numerous as the stars in the sky.

The details in the two stories are fascinating. It was as if a script was repeating itself from one generation to the next. Moreover, you see this reality of family scripts in the stories of the kings of Israel and Judah. The Scriptures describe twelve of the twenty kings of Judah as evil, idolatrous, and sinful. When these kings are mentioned and their actions indicted, we often find a phrase that goes something like "He did evil in the eyes of the Lord, just as his father had done" (e.g. 1 Kings 15:3, 26; 22:52). When the actions of the good kings are described, they are accompanied by phrases like "just as his father had done" (2 Kings 15:3, 34). Or "just as his [fore]father David had done" (2 Kings 18:3). The therapeutic world may have put an actual label on it, but the reality of unwritten family scripts has existed since the beginning of time. These relational scripts may not be proven in a test lab. They may not be documented as laws of physics. But they are real nonetheless. And I propose the reality of scripts plays out even more ...

If every church is a family, then specific to every church is a family script. But rather than involving behaviors like alcoholism, suicide, or domestic violence, a church's script has to do with its own unwritten modes of Christian behavior: how to pray, read the Bible, worship, evangelize, counsel, even communicate.

A writer for *GQ* magazine, John Jeremiah Sullivan, wrote an article titled "Upon This Rock," documenting a road trip he took to the 2004 Creation Festival. The Creation Festival draws approximately one hundred thousand Christians, mostly evangelical teenagers, there to see their favorite Christian bands. So Sullivan posted an invitation on a couple of forums at YouthOnTheRock.com to join him for a road trip from Manhattan to Lake of the Ozarks, where the festival was to be held. His aim—"I wanted to know what these people are, who claim to love this music, who drive hundreds of miles, traversing states, to hear it live."[2] Thank God the folks on the website keep an eye out for potentially shady characters, because his post was deleted from the forums and no one picked up on his offer (fearing he may be a pedophile). So he went alone.

At times, Sullivan's observations are poignant, like when he detailed the demographic he found there:

> The Evangelical strata were more or less recognizable from my high school days, though everyone, I observed, had gotten better looking. Lots were dressed like skate punks or in last season's East Village couture (nondenominationals); others were fairly trailer (rural Baptists or Church of God); there were preps (Young Life, Fellowship of Christian Athletes—these were the ones who'd have the pot). You could spot the stricter sectarians right away, their unchanging antifashion and pale glum faces. When I asked one woman, later, how many she reckoned were white, she said, "Roughly 100 percent."[3]

Or when Sullivan described the festival's music scene, he explained, "Remember those perfume dispensers they used to have in pharmacies—'If you like Drakkar Noir, you'll love Sexy Musk'? Well, Christian rock works like that."[4]

But after spending time with a few particular guys throughout the week, Sullivan was given a distinct impression of their character. He depicted his companions for the week as genuinely compassionate, relating and communicating not out of anger but love. Toward the end of the week, Sullivan was walking with Darius, Ritter, and Bub when something happened to him. He was a long way off from the stage but could see well enough to notice the middle-aged guys on stage with "blousy shirts" and "arena-rock moves from the mid-'80s." Sullivan started wondering, what is this feeling?—while the singer kept grinning between lines. He said, "I could just make out the words":

> There's a higher place to go
> (beyond belief, beyond belief)
> Where we reach the next plateau,
> (beyond belief, beyond belief) ...

Suddenly, the straw he'd been chewing on slipped from his mouth as he said, "Oh @#%&*, it's Petra." Immediately, a phase from his past came to mind. They were a few particular years from high school that he spent as part of a nondenominational church after having been invited by his friend, Verm. Sullivan had developed a friendship with Verm after the two learned they were both fans of The Smiths. They exchanged tapes and started hanging out quite a bit. "Then the moment came that always comes when you make friends with a born-again: 'Listen, I go to this thing on Wednesday nights. It's like a Bible study—no, listen, it's cool. The people are actually really cool.'"[5]

To his amazement, they really were. At the time, all his ideas about Christians fell by the wayside. They were accepting people, who seemed quite eager and loaded with a defense for every question Sullivan had about Christianity. Before long, he "prayed the prayer" and was a full-fledged member of the church and youth group. He and Verm even began leading a Bible study, going to conferences and retreats, taking theology classes, as well as attending cell group meetings every week on Friday or Saturday nights.

Eventually, Sullivan met up with a higher-ranked leader in the church known as "Mole" and described his tutelage under Mole like this:

> Cell group was typically held in somebody's dining room, somebody pretty high up in the group. You have to understand what an honor it was to be in a cell with Mole. People would see me at central meeting and be like, "How is that, getting to rap with him every week?" It was awesome. He really got down with the Word (he had a wonderful old hippie way of talking; everything was something action: "time for some fellowship action ... let's get some chips 'n' salsa action"). He carried a

> heavy "study Bible"—no King James for the non-denominationals; too many inaccuracies. When he cracked open its hand-tooled leather cover, you knew it was on. And no joke: The brother was gifted. Even handicapped by the relatively pedestrian style of the New American Standard version, he could twist a verse into your conscience like a bone screw, make you think Christ was standing there nodding approval.[6]

Hilarious.

For Christians, this article should summon a mixture of responses. Sullivan's festival experience and recollection of his church days deal a serious blow to the subtitles of Christian church life. My guess is, if he actually tried, Sullivan could slip right back into the system with perfect fluency (having spent a few years inside the church himself). After all, he didn't need much explanation for some of our mainstay Christian norms. Outfit him with a "heavy study Bible" and a few phrases like "action," "pray the prayer," and "get down with the Word," and you've got a full-on local in many church settings.

In other words, our Christian subculture has created its own scripts—its own means of instructing others (verbally or non-verbally) on how to do the things we as Christians do ... pray, worship, read the Bible, counsel, even how to be caring and how to forgive. These scripts cycle from one generation to the next. Most often, they are unwritten. However, there are times when they're actually taught. At times they are scripts unto themselves, one for each Christian part—one for prayer, one for worship, one for Bible reading, one for adequately consoling a friend. And each is lying on a table just looking for an actor to come along and play the part.

In this world, I've achieved Russell Crowe status. At times, you can't tell the difference between the character I'm playing and the person I truly am. After Jamie Foxx's performance in *Ray*, I overheard someone say, "When I saw the real Ray Charles during the credits at the end of the film, I thought, Who is *that* guy? Foxx had done such an outstanding job, I thought he *was* Ray." And for some of us, the performance of Christianity is no different. With the right vocabulary, mannerisms, and external accessories, we increase our chances of acting. The more familiar we become with our lines and looks, the greater the possibility for theater.

How do you worship God? Stand up. Sing songs of praise to God. Close your eyes. Raise your hands to the sky.

Within different church settings, the raised hands have become an exact science. Whole levels of spirituality are derived from the placement or extension of the hands. Levels of meaning are attached to how tightly the eyes are clinched.

Or how do you read the Bible? Select a book of the Bible. Pray to God for illumination. Read the chapter. Pick out certain words or phrases to study in depth. Cross-reference such words with other passages of Scripture using the same word(s). Deduce logical meaning from such words. Conclude with applications for today's world.

Lose the idea that Scripture was meant to missionally read you, rather than you mechanistically read it. Place a text from the Bible into a lifeless, rigid outline where notes have been scribbled and applications drawn, and supposedly Scripture has been engaged.

Instead, allow Scripture to become a member of the local church community where the sacred text functions as a living organism that baffles, mystifies, affirms, confuses, and convicts.

Rather than standing over Scripture to divide and conquer, we sit beneath it with intrigue.

How do you communicate concern to another person during conversation? Establish eye contact. Focus the conversation on them, asking more questions about their well-being than they ask you. Repeat what they just said back in sympathetic tone. Advanced level: Read a Scripture verse to them pertaining to their situation.

This is an easy formula. If the number of questions posed to them is greater than the number of questions asked of you, genuine concern for their well-being has been accomplished. Lose the fact that genuine curiosity can't be faked.

And, of course, how should you pray? Address God as "Father God." Begin by thanking Him for five to seven things or people around you. Use the word "just" a minimum of twenty-five times. At the beginning of each new phrase or sentence, address God again as "Father God" (to ensure He hasn't forgotten who's being addressed). Staple every ending with, "In the name of Jesus we pray. Amen."

Keep in mind, more emotion, greater number of words, and increased volume equal more meaning. Shed the possibility that prayer could actually be used for the promotion of self. Simply increase the level of emotion, the volume, and the number of words used, and enjoy pure and free connection with God. (Admittedly, I agree with what G.K. Chesterton said at one time, that the test of a good religion is whether you can joke about it.)

This is why I've always been suspicious of any pastor or Bible study leader who provides detailed instruction to others on how to situate the externals—the degree of elevation in hand placement, certain words guaranteed to reach the stratosphere, the configuration of the physical body to transport the person to another world.

UPOKRISEUS

In Matthew's Gospel account, chapter 23 finds Jesus indicting the scribes and Pharisees for acting like frauds. At one point, Jesus compared them to white-washed tombs, no doubt a provocative image for religious experts accustomed only to hearing praise.

Tombs in the first century were above the ground. Jews kept their distance from tombs because contact with these graves made them ritually unclean. Therefore, the tombs were washed white so as to be easily noticed by Jews. Ironically, then, you had beautiful monuments on the outside that were full of bones and death on the inside.

Being the good rabbi that He was with a mind for creating powerful imagery, Jesus also associated the Pharisees with the Greek word *upokriseus* (verses 13-29). The literal rendering for this word would be "hypocrite"; however, Jesus' first-century audience wouldn't have interpreted "hypocrite" as we do today. Today, two thousand years later, we hear the word "hypocrite" and immediately think "two-faced." One who says one thing but does another. One who talks the talk but doesn't walk the walk. But that's not the leap Jesus' hearers in the first century would have immediately made.

In the ancient world, Jesus' audience would have simply thought "actor." One who plays a part on a stage. That is, for the average first-century Roman citizen, Jesus says *upokriseus,* and instantly His hearers are mentally taken to a local Roman stage involving costumes, performances, and acting troupes. This, to be precise, is what Jesus indicted the Pharisees for being! They had achieved such proficiency in their religious practices that their teachings had begun rotating around the skills, methods, and techniques of following God rather than the seat of all movement (the heart). Their lines were unattached from their person.

To my knowledge, the only demographic of people today who don't know a thing about acting are children. For better or worse, they're the only species of human beings who don't have it in 'em to create an impression that's just not there. They—or at least *mine*—don't have a clue how not to scream out a thought the instant it strikes the brain. For better or worse.

I vividly remember a Sunday lunch not too long ago when our family was sitting at a long table of church friends and my four-year-old blurted out the fact that she didn't have a fork. Unfortunately, she could not yet pronounce her R's. So when everyone else began wondering how I'd taught my daughter to drop the f-bomb, she was completely unaware.

I've also experienced Avery pointing at a large unpregnant woman standing about six feet away in the grocery store and yelling, "Look, Daddy, that lady has a baby in her belly!"—I felt like opening my wallet, turning to the lady, and repenting, "My bad, how much will that cost me?"

Still, topping my list have been the daily elemental questions Avery has asked over the past year. As a child (and a female child at that), she moves through her day engrossed in every moment, often trading emotion for every interval of time. Every interval I tell you. No exaggeration. By breakfast, I'm worn out. The split second she encounters a word or phrase that doesn't register, a word or phrase she's never heard before, she turns it to question.

"Daddy, what does 'matter of fact' mean?"

"Daddy, what is 'consequences'?"

"Daddy, how many Doras is that? Is it one Dora or two Doras?" Avery's understanding of time operates within the framework of one *Dora the Explorer* episode (thirty minutes). So when she asks questions involving quantity, she references "Dora" as the standard.

"Daddy, what does 'might as well' mean?"
(ad infinitum)

The beautiful thing about children is that they've not yet been given the lines. No preconceived ideas. They've not yet seen the template for conducting themselves as interested, caring, or intelligent individuals. They only know one way to be. Themselves.

When Avery and I have conversation, she doesn't know how to *act* interested. When she asks questions, she doesn't know how to *act* curious. She simply is or she isn't. It's clear as day. She's not conscious of appearing stupid, nor is she conscious of coming across disinterested. But do you know what is the most beautiful aspect of all? She's not conscious of how spiritual or religious she is coming across. There's never a time in the day when the thought floats through her head, "Am I coming across humble here?" Or "That guy is going through a difficult time. I better sound sympathetic." For the little time she has in life like this, I relish her blatant transparency. I soak up every "what does that mean" like I'm starved for it.

It is in our conversations with God that I think the unfiltered way of a child provides clear, unmistakable direction. Surely, prayer is what happens when you are no longer conscious of how you look or how you sound. It is the uninhibited space where costumes and scripts are laid aside. Especially religious ones. Ironically, if we are serious about following Christ, I would propose that the number one part we as Christians must sacrifice on a daily basis is the script of spirituality. It is the desire to scale spiritual heights—to become the next super-spiritual heavyweight—that has the greatest potential to pull us away from the actual following of Christ.

Brennan Manning explains this most vulnerably.

> Dishonesty disowns my true identity as Abba's child and allows my false self, the impostor who is the slick, sick and sinister impersonator of my true self, to engage life on a fraudulent basis. I have lionized my accomplishments in ministry with self-deprecating humor to create the impression that I am humble; I have vaunted my gift of discernment, insisting with false modesty that the gift must be attributed to others; I have manifested extraordinary pseudo-serenity in the face of adversity, and meekly protested about the burdens of leadership. Each ploy is designed to fasten attention to myself.[7]

Unfortunately, this is the cinematic experience I know all too well. I may not have a future in front of a camera, but I'm well versed in posturing humility, discernment, false modesty, pseudo-serenity, meekness, and the list goes on. Every bit of it "designed to fasten attention to myself."

It's when our prayer lives have no thought of spiritual upward mobility that we begin to actually find our way. Jesus communicated this very thing in a culture that placed women and children at the bottom of the social totem pole. The disciples had asked Him the question, "Who gets the highest rank in God's kingdom?" "For an answer Jesus called over a child, whom he stood in the middle of the room, and said, 'I'm telling you, once and for all, that unless you return to square one and start over like children, you're not even going to get a look at the kingdom, let alone get in. Whoever becomes simple and elemental again, like this child, will rank high in God's kingdom'" (Matt. 18:2-4, MSG).

AVOIDING AUTOPILOT

There is an aspect of our life in prayer, then, that demands an inward attentiveness to words and behaviors cloaked in spirituality. In order for us to be people of truth from the inside out, we must develop a constant suspicion toward the very thing in which we're involved—religion. For this reason, I suggest the abandonment of all insider language and spiritual clichés while praying.

Insider language is vocabulary that's become common knowledge for a specific group of people but is largely unknown or incomprehensible by those outside the group. It's a powerful tool of communication among those within the organization because it fuels the cohesion of the team. It distinguishes who's in and who's out and even has the potential to elevate those most fluent in the lingo.

I used to think insider language was confined strictly to use among evangelical Christians, until recently. I was at Best Buy satisfying my newfound addiction—perusing the latest HDTVs—when I noticed something disturbing on several of the sets. On the actual frame of the TV, right there staring me in the face in metallic lettering, was a string of coded specs: DLP DNIe 720p. What in the blazes? You mean to tell me that if I were to purchase this TV and develop the sort of intimate romance with her that I intend, I would have DLP DNIe 720p in the bottom right-hand panel corner just below the screen? Every single time I watched TV? It's like they've taken a perfectly well-designed hot fudge sundae and sprinkled chopped spinach on top.

What would ever possess the manufacturers of this HDTV to fix DLP DNIe 720p on the flippin' front of it? Why not just center the brand name along the bottom panel just below the screen and create a clean, unencumbered, visually stunning masterpiece? Evidently, this information was viewed as vital to the purchasing process in the hopes that someone like me walking the aisle at Best Buy would pass this particular set, be stopped in their tracks, and say, "Whoa, whoa, whoa! This one comes with a Digital Light Processing chip and a Digital Natural Imagine engine that incorporates noise reduction while delivering enhanced contrast, white level, and picture detail! Nuh-uh, it even delivers 720 lines vertically scanned in a progressive fashion! Done deal!"

My unofficial poll results tells me there aren't too many consumers with this level of knowledge, yet it was deemed vital enough to be slapped on the front—not the back or side—of a TV. Only the purest HDTV connoisseurs would have any clue as to what this means. Apparently, insider language takes place outside of evangelical Christianity as well. In truth, it exists in just about every organization or location where a group of people gather for a common purpose—businesses, clubs, teams, and churches alike.

You play golf? Then you must be familiar with a few terms like backdoor, four-jack, grow teeth, in the leather, kick, knee-knocker, run, and thin.

Backdoor—The part of the cup located opposite the ball on the green. To reach the backdoor, a putt must curl around most of the hole before dropping in.

Four-jack—To take four putts on a hole. Only tolerable for those who can drive the green on a par five.

Grow teeth—A golfer's plea for the ball to stop quickly.

In the leather—Phrase meaning a putt is close enough to the cup (a distance no greater than the length of the putter grip) to be conceded.

Kick—Literally, the way the ball bounces. Sometimes it kicks your way and sometimes it doesn't, but golfers are always asking for a good kick.

Knee-knocker—A putt in the three- to four-foot range. The term comes from the nervous trembling that accompanies these short putts.

Run—Whenever the ball is moving along the ground, it is said to be running.

Thin—To hit the ball in the center with the club's leading edge, instead of sliding under it. Chances are your shot will fly lower and farther than you intended. This is still much better than hitting it fat.

Or you work as a barista. Or maybe you're just addicted to coffee like me. Then you're familiar with words like acidity, body, depth charge, doppio, draw, drip, dry cappuccino, flat, group,

group head, knockbox, lungo, pull, red eye, ristretto, short, short shot, skinny, straight shot, tamping, wet cappuccino, and with legs.

Acidity—The crispness of the coffee that provides a sharp, bright, vibrant quality. The taste of freshness. It is the sensation of dryness that the coffee produces under the edges of your tongue and on the back of your palate.

Body—The weight of the coffee on your tongue. The heaviness, viscosity, thickness, or richness that you perceive on your tongue, similar to whole milk. It could range from full (buttery and syrupy) to medium to light.

Depth charge—A cup of coffee with a shot of espresso.

Doppio—A double shot of espresso.

Draw—To prepare an espresso shot. (See also Pull.)

Drip—Short for drip-brewed coffee.

Dry cappuccino—A cappuccino with foam only, no steamed milk.

Flat—No foam.

Group—An espresso machine's brewing chamber, comprising the group head and the portafilter.

Group head—The circular unit that forms the upper half of an espresso machine's brewing chamber and into which the barista places the portafilter.

Knockbox—A container with a padded bar across the top for the barista to use to "knock" the brewed coffee grounds out of the portafilter.

Lungo—A long shot of espresso, about one to two ounces per seven grams of coffee.

Pull—Used as a verb to describe the act of making espresso, as in "to pull a shot."

Red eye—Same as Depth charge.

Ristretto—A shot of espresso that is cut off at fifteen to twenty seconds (when the crema turns light brown) yielding less than one ounce per seven grams of coffee; an aficionado's ambrosia.

Short—An eight-ounce serving of coffee or espresso drink.

Short shot—Also Short pull. Same as Ristretto.

Skinny—An espresso drink made with nonfat milk.

Straight shot—An espresso served without milk, steamed milk, or foam; the drink of true purists.

Tamping—The action of packing the coffee into the portafilter with enough force to ensure the proper extraction.

Wet cappuccino—A cappuccino with foam and steamed milk; usually the espresso, foam, and steamed milk are in a 1:1:1 ratio.

With legs—A drink to go.

Personally, I don't think the use of insider language is beneficial for the overall practice of the church, but my reasons for excluding it from prayer life are specifically different than my reasons for excluding it from church life and especially its use in everyday living.

While in the car on the way to a meeting I had felt apprehensive about for several days, I began talking to God about it, and almost without thinking, I voiced, "God, I place this meeting in Your hands." As soon as this phrase left my mouth, I realized the clichéd vibe of my conversation with God and questioned, "Wait, what do I mean by that?" I've prayed those very words for years and years, but I think my feelings about that phrase have changed over time—from what I meant by that phrase five years ago to what I mean by that phrase now ...

Rather than allowing myself to continue on the path of usual conversation with God, I stopped to process my words and motives to God aloud:

> God, when I say "I place this meeting in Your hands," You know that I don't expect this meeting to come off without a hitch just because I've "given it to You." I know that Your involvement in my life doesn't guarantee unwavering success, and it certainly doesn't guar-

antee that things will turn out just as I want them to. There are other people involved here who may have entirely different views and hopes than I do.

God, Your thoughts and Your ways are far beyond mine.

You are probably aware of what I want to see happen here. I really hope we'll get on the other side of this meeting, and everyone will be on the same page. And if there are disagreements, I hope they'll be worked out smoothly. But, God, I know that's not always the way things turn out. Help me do my part in creating a constructive environment and to communicate clearly, respectfully, and with definite boundaries.

I guess, in the end, what I'm saying is that I'm not placing this meeting in Your hands just so I don't have to take responsibility for how it turns out. And I'm also not placing this meeting in Your hands just to finagle the outcome I want.

But I do know You have my best interests in mind, and that You're not working against me, but for me. So help me keep trusting You and Your desires for my life.

In other words, if you've spent any length of time in a church setting, then truthful speech will demand some serious excavation. You must be willing to locate and uncover the scripts that have been handed down for generations in regard to the way you should pray, what you should say, which words and phrases can supposedly travel the greatest distance. The irony here is that many times those who've lived the majority of their lives outside of the church have an easier time being truthful than those from within.

Take "be with" for instance. ("Lord, be with Lucy as she goes into surgery." "Be with Bob today as he buries himself to the neck in pickles.") What is that? Didn't Jesus say, "I am with you *always*." Do we have to ask Him to do something He's already always doing?

What I think we're usually asking is that people would be extra aware of the fact that God is with them while they go through whatever. So why don't we just say that?

Another one is "bless." ("Lord, bless Taleshia." "Lord, bless this service." "Bless us with no mountain lions at this wedding.") Where, besides praying, do we talk like that? "Yes, I'd like you to bless me with a #1 Combo, monstro-sized, no onions, please." "Thanks for calling Technocorp, how may I bless you?" It's almost like it's become a generic word for every situation. How wonderful it must be to the ears of God to hear our generic conversations with Him.

Then there's my favorite: "lead, guide, and direct." This is the one that usually signals to the listener that the prayer is over since it is almost always the last thing said. ("... and we ask that you lead, guide, and direct this pedicure. Amen.") Let's see: Lead. Guide. Direct. Three words that all mean exactly the same thing. Why don't we use multiple synonyms in other parts of the prayer? Why just at the end? Why just those three words? We could easily pray "bless, bolster, and support" or "heal, fix, and patch up" since apparently God didn't know what we meant the first time.

It really is a challenge (for me, anyway) to avoid using worn-out autopilot phrases when talking to God. Try it.

> The next time you're called on to pray for something in a group, do it without using the word "bless." It'll almost drive you nuts. You'll want to say it so bad, you'll be shaking violently just trying to restrain yourself. And then everyone will just think you're super-spiritual—praying and shaking. It's a little known fact that Benny Hinn actually has no effect on people other than being able to stop them from saying "lead, guide, and direct." That's what you're really seeing on TV. So we should cut the Christianese. But slowly, okay? No need to hurt, assail, or besiege yourself.[8]

With this in mind, I suggest a list of words that need to be mined for meaning. This list is by no means exhaustive. In fact, I wonder how many more words and phrases you could add? In offering this list, I have operated by this rule of thumb: If I can't use other "real-life" words to articulate what I'm saying, there's a good chance I don't know what I mean or for what I'm actually praying.

(as stated)
Place in Your hands
Be with
Bless
Lead, guide, and direct

Fellowship—What do we mean here ... friendship?

In the word—What word? Any word? How about the word "amanuensis"? Or what about the word "solipsism"? Or "gourmand"? Any of these words will do, and I aim to get in them tonight for several minutes, or maybe in the morning. It's usually preferable if

I get in "amanuensis" in the morning, but I guess the evening will do.

Confess—Acknowledge? Admit? Say? Communicate?

Repent—Technically, this biblical word has to do with steering your life in the opposite direction from where it was originally headed. So why not communicate just that?

Born again—Need I say more?

Have a burden—Is it heavy?

The lost—Rule of thumb: references to a group of people that could come across disrespectful or demeaning shouldn't have any place in our conversations, whether conversations with God or conversations with friends. A possible alternative: "people outside of the church."

Anointed/anointing—Could this term be just another way in which very human Christians create spiritual hierarchy where there are always some better than others? In the Gospel accounts, if Jesus ever elevated or distinguished anyone, it was most often a person rarely considered to be "spiritual" in the eyes of others.

Raise up—Instruct others along a certain path? Bring others along in the way of Christ?

Prosper you/me—A term that needs some serious rethinking. "Prosper" as in "financially prosper"? It seems as though there is a difference between God providing for our needs and (what has been dubbed) "The Health & Wealth Gospel" that is preached with vast regularity. The confusion here, though, is understandable. Deuteronomic Law preached the H&WG—that is, follow God and experience "blessing" (better health, more money, victory in battle, good harvest). Then as the Old Testament unfolds, we see an inner dialogue take shape between Job, the prophets, and the Deuteronomic Law—where people experience illness and suffering as a result of following God. By the time Jesus comes on the scene, the H&WG is blown out of the water. There is no perception whatsoever that following Jesus will reap a plush life. (Reference the lives of the disciples, Paul writing from prison cells, and the book of Acts where suffering was always imminent and somewhat expected.) Summarily, the desire for provision is a human one, but the place where provision becomes wealth should always be questioned.

We call on you to ...—From where is God being "called"? A remote location apart from God's presence? Where is that? Or is this prelude intended to create more emphasis? Like, "God, okay, now this next part of the prayer I really want badly, so I'm going to put it in italics ..."

Create a hedge of protection around ...—A "hedge"? I thought "hedges" were clipped?

Of course, we ask all this only if it be Your will—For your consideration, what exactly is a "will"? Perhaps this very term demands the most negotiation of any. How does the dictionary define "will" and how exact is God's "will" for your life?

Go before us and ...—We need Einstein for this one, literally. Albert Einstein, physicist (1879-1955). Are we not talking about the basic principles that govern the structure and behavior of matter? Are we not literally saying, "Go before us *in time* and ..."? As in, "Dear Lord, Go before us in time and prepare the path that lays before us. Well, God, come to think of it, I guess I'm asking You to time travel. Ya know, if You wouldn't mind traveling in the forward flow of movement as close to the speed of light as possible, that'd be great. And when You get there, could You pave my way so my circumstances will be nice and pleasurable? (yawn) I'm not really asking You to travel into the past, because history would just get alllll screwed up. I mean, what would I study in school? Heck, how far back would You go? (yawn, yawn) Would it screw up the Bible? Well, I could be going off on a tangent here, God. Hmmm, this shouldn't be too difficult for YOU since You exist outside of time and all ... but

```
if You time traveled, would that affect
the events of the present if ... Zzzzz,
Zzzzz, Zzzzz ..."
```

I've always had difficulty with clichés anyway, mixing my metaphors as they say. I just never seem to get them right. "Take the bull by the hand" (bull by the horns). "Let's keep that under tabs" (keep it under wraps/keep tabs on it). "Oh, that's smoke under the bridge" (water under the bridge, smoke and mirrors). "Make sure we're all on the same playing field" (level the playing field/all on the same page). "I don't know if we can stay above water" (stay afloat/keep our heads above water).

It just seems about time someone started mixing their Christian clichés. Maybe you'd be up for this. Next time you're in a church group setting, perhaps you could play with this a little ... What if you volunteered to pray? The more inopportune time, the better—like in the very middle of discussion. Who in their right mind would argue this suggestion? Then, in your best spiritual tone, interject, *"Why don't we just pray about that?"*

Once you've successfully lowered each head in the group, keep one eye open and begin praying. Somewhere along the way, feel free to incorporate, "Please, God, create a hedge of anointing around ... " and "We place this in Your head." Then just before closing out your prayer say, "And we ask that You lead, guide, and confess us. Amen." Again, you've got to remember to keep one eye open so you're able to notice whether your mixed metaphors have affected anyone in the least. Of course, that eye will also help inform you when you've crossed over into hell for doing such things.

Obviously, my aim here has been to unload some of the words and phrases that have been employed far too long. My fear: that 90 percent of our communication with God has become cliché, a subconscious crutch. My target: simple conversation with God where tired, vacant language is abandoned and replaced with truthful speech.

Interestingly enough, the etymology of the word "true" finds an ancient connection with the word "tree." "In Old English, the words looked and sounded much more alike than they do now: 'Tree' was *tro^{e}w* and 'true' was *tro^{e}we*."[9] "Truth" could be regarded as having a sense of rooted firmness. In other words, the sort of truthful speech we're striving for in conversation with God ought to plumb the depths of who we are.

CLOSING THOUGHTS

I realize some come to this conversation having experienced a spiritual burnout at some point in their past (or perhaps are currently in the middle of one). Spiritual burnout can take hold for a number of reasons. It could happen as a result of a massive paradigm shift where a previously held theological system got demolished in the blink of an eye. Or spiritual burnout could happen when the outer person—the person others see who shows up for work, school, church, even prayer—becomes completely detached from their interior person. Or it could happen when someone has placed the exterior, peripheral aspects of following Christ into the center and made them function as *the thing*. The thing that gives life to the full.

I doubt I could adequately speak of spiritual burnout if I had not experienced it deeply myself. What I find most discouraging about it, though, is that someone could walk into church off the streets and discover a level of freedom in Christ where the grace of God has taken hold, and then five minutes later be loaded down with a new religious song and dance and a new religious language promised to take them to spiritual heights. It's as if they've just unloaded their own set of Samsonites only to trade them in for the religious version—made of a durable nylon/polyester blend with a sleek spiritual finish, but every bit as heavy as the previous load. No wonder so many people within the church experience spiritual burnout.

Perhaps Christ brings rescue not just to those loaded down with addictions, greed, lust, and self-absorption, but even to those loaded down with religion. After all, He did say, "Are you tired? Worn out? Burned out on religion? Come to me. Get away with me and you'll recover your life. I'll show you how to take a real rest. Walk with me and work with me—watch how I do it. Learn the unforced rhythms of grace. I won't lay anything heavy or ill-fitting on you. Keep company with me and you'll learn to live freely and lightly" (Matt. 11:28-30, MSG).

7
CHAPTER
RECIPE THEOLOGY

Go to Amazon.com. Type in "7 Steps To" and hit enter. This is what you'll find:

- *7 Steps to Emotional Intelligence* by Patrick E. Merlevede, Denis Bridoux, and Rudy Vandamme
- *7-Step System to Building a $1,000,000 Network Marketing Dynasty* by Joe Rubino
- *7 Steps to Overcoming Anxiety and Depression* by Gary Null
- *7 Steps to a Pain-Free Life* by Robin McKenzie and Craig Kubey
- *7 Steps to Bible Skills* by Dorothy Hellstern
- *7 Steps to Fearless Speaking* by Lilyan Wilder
- *7 Steps to Bonding with Your Stepchild* by Suzen J. Ziegahn
- *7 Steps to Perfect Health* by Gary Null
- *7 Steps to a Smoke-Free Life* by Edwin B. Fisher
- *Your Best Life Now: 7 Steps to Living at Your Full Potential* by Joel Osteen
- *7 Easy Steps to CNC Programming ... A Beginner's Guide* by David Hayden

- 7 *Steps to Normal Bladder Control* by Elizabeth Vierck
- 7 *Steps to Success Trading Options Online* by Larry D. Spears
- 7 *Steps to Passionate Love* by William Van Horn
- 7 *Steps to Freedom* II by Benjamin D. Suarez
- 7 *Steps to Successful Selling* by Traci Bild and Todd Shafer

And those are just the first several listings of 774.

Who in their right mind isn't the least bit lured by a step-by-step instructional, get-down-to-brass-tax, tell-you-how-to-do-it prescription for navigating life? Did you just say, "Not me"? Liar! The promise of certainty is unparalleled in today's society and always will be. Isn't that what a "recipe" is in the first place? "A method of doing or treating something that relies on an established, uncontroversial model or approach."[1] In other words, someone somewhere has tested a particular set of behaviors X number of times and discovered a certain result every single time (or almost every single time). According to the recipes mentioned earlier, someone has discovered a seven-step program for experiencing passionate love, overcoming anxiety and depression, bonding with your stepchild, gaining control of your bladder, or learning Bible skills.

To be fair, we've been hard-wired this way. The Seven Steps To—Three Rules Of—Five Factors marketing scheme hasn't been around forever. I'd have a hard time believing Saint Bernard of Clairvaux ever preached a sermon in the twelfth century titled, "The Seven Steps to Successful Fasting and Prayer." We live in the machine age, a technological world.

Think about it. What chance do you possibly have of making it out your door in the morning without first coming into contact with some sort of mechanical device? Virtually every minute of every day demands our interaction with a contraption of screws, bolts, springs, wires, plastic, cables, and running electricity. Unless you're Amish, of course.

From the moment you rise, every device is waiting to be operated, turned, controlled, moved, and maneuvered. From the alarm clock to the light switch, the toilet to the shower knobs, the remote control to the TiVo, the toaster oven to the coffee maker. And that's before you've even left the house.

You duck your head and step inside your car. Insert the key into the ignition and turn it to the right. The ignition circuit takes the voltage from the battery and sends it to the proper spark plug at the proper time to cause the air/fuel mixture in that cylinder to explode near the top of its travel ... Blah, blah, blah, so on, so forth ... and in the blink of an eye, the vehicle starts up.

All machines hinge on this single premise: You do X and the machine does Y. You push the lever, and the commode flushes. You turn the knob, and out comes running water. You clap, and the lights come on. But those are machines. Not people. And certainly not God. Author and professor Larry Crabb said many times we approach God in the same sort of mechanistic way. "We're all tempted to expect God to do B if we do A. If we've been 'good enough' in some area, surely God will be at least 'good enough' back, no?"[2] Call it "recipe theology." Pray a certain prayer, perform a good deed, live a good life, fast, and all the while solidify the outcome you want. Crabb said, "We want the general principles from the Book of Proverbs to work every time in every situation. We want our spouses, for example, to respond the way we want them to when we speak their 'love language.'"[3]

Crabb's students often nodded in agreement as they noticed their own attempts at living by formulas. As they were praying, one student blurted out with a laugh as someone said, "O, God, I even want to be broken *right*!" And not only do we want to be "broken *right*," we also want to be humble *right*, empathize *right*, encourage *right*, actively listen *right*, and worship *right*.

Some have even turned Sunday worship gatherings into a prescription for experiencing God's presence. They've turned passages like Psalm 22:3 into a recipe, saying, "God, the Scriptures say that You inhabit the praises of Your people. Well, let's get to praising so You'll 'show up'!" They've mistakenly taken Psalm 22:3 to mean that we as humans can pull the strings on how, when, and where God "shows up"—as if we can literally cause God to sit down and remain in our presence by singing songs and hymns of praise. (Matthew 18:20—"For where two or three come together in my name, there am I with them"—has evoked similar sentiments.)

But in the Scriptures, from beginning to end, there seems to be a clear-cut distinction regarding who plays the role of God. A few arguments ensue from time to time. Even a wrestling match or two. But God is left standing every time. When God is asked by Moses to identify Himself in Exodus 3:13-14, He refuses to be pigeon-holed with one characterization ... Love ... Justice ... Power ... Forgiveness ... Grace ... Wrath. God doesn't respond to Moses by giving a name. In fact, the literal Hebrew phrase that God uses to identify Himself is "I am who I am."

Some will try their darnedest to treat God as they do their toaster oven, but He'll have none of it. He can't be manipulated or controlled. Life seems to work the same way. Completely unpredictable no matter who you are (Christian or not).
For instance, drunk drivers aren't particularly picky about the belief systems of the people they hit. Or what about the co-worker who got three hours of sleep the night before. He lacks a sufficient level of alertness and drops the ball on a key item at work which sets off a chain reaction ... next thing you know, the weekend you planned eight weeks in advance has now been royally screwed up. Try controlling that.

If you really want to ensure 100 percent certainty in creating the outcomes you want, you'll need to somehow manipulate a few things. For starters: the sleep patterns, diets, amount of knowledge, attitudes, schedules, and thought processes made by every person you come in contact with in a given day; a climate conducive to your goals—clear skies/75°/8mph wind/40 percent humidity or overcast/25°/light snow; the amount of allergens in your immediate environment; your own mood, diet, thought processes, and amount of sleep; viruses and illnesses potentially passed from one individual to the next in your immediate five-mile radius; Internet connectivity; traffic; and, of course, the choices made by you and those around you.

BUT, BUT, BUT ...

Some say, "But it says it right there in the Bible, 'And all things you ask in prayer, believing, you will receive' (Matt. 21:22, NAS). What gives? And what about, 'Ask, and it will be given to you; seek, and you will find; knock, and it will be opened to you' (Matt. 7:7, NAS)? Sounds pretty cause-and-effect to me! Sounds very much like X's and Y's, A's and B's—you do this, God will do that—recipe theology right in front of our eyes!"

Matthew 21:22 has always been a bit of a mystery to me. How could Jesus indict the Pharisees for treating the Jewish Law like an algorithm, then turn around and create one of His own?

Others say, "If you just have enough belief, you'll be able to have whatever you want. Increasing the level of faith to exponential quotients equals your desired outcome through prayer." Could this be right?

Keep in mind, a huge disservice to Scripture takes place any time we take a verse or teaching and try to lift it out from its setting without any connection to the milieu or historical context in which the passage comes. God's Word always comes to us in context. It's always a message that comes to people in a particular time and a particular place with certain needs and challenges.

Matthew 21:22 follows a story about the cleansing of the Jewish temple where Jesus had previously cleared all mercantile activity (Matt. 21:12-17). The Jewish temple was the physical center of the Jewish faith. While there, Jesus not only cleared it of all moneymaking businesses but also healed the blind and the lame. So, in cleansing the temple, Jesus not only points to one of the symptoms of Israel's failure in its covenant relationship with Yahweh, but His act also points to the real presence of the kingdom of God (Jesus Himself).

Israel saw herself to be the centerpiece of what the Creator God was doing and would do for the world as a whole, but Jesus as prophet enters the scene and is ushering in a new world order where the stage is not built around the Jewish temple. In fact, the temple is under judgment as Christ is building a new temple, so to speak, one that is open to the public and takes root in people's hearts.

Then, this odd story follows the cleansing of the temple:

> Early the next morning Jesus was returning to the city. He was hungry. Seeing a lone fig tree alongside the road, he approached it anticipating a breakfast of figs. When he got to the tree, there was nothing but fig leaves. He said, "No more figs from this tree—ever!" The fig tree withered on the spot, a dry stick. The disciples saw it happen. They rubbed their eyes, saying, "Did we really see this? A leafy tree one minute, a dry stick the next?" (Matt. 21:18-20, MSG)

When I read this, I immediately think, "Jesus must not have been a morning person!" Or maybe He was hypoglycemic? Yes, He was hypoglycemic. That's the only possible explanation for why in the blazes Jesus would have hauled off and unloaded on a woody trunk and a few branches. It makes no other sense. His blood-sugar level was extremely low, so His patience was already wearing thin. Nature's waiter brings out a plate full of air, so He pulverizes the restaurant. Yep, that's it. Low blood-sugar.

But N.T. Wright explains that the cleansing of the temple and the cursing of the fig tree aren't just coincidentally held in the same chapter. The cleansing of the temple signifies a new world order and judgment on Israel's constant unfaithfulness. Wright says that there are some strange events in the New Testament that echo this fact—the cursing of the fig tree being one of them.

In other words, just as the tree was unfruitful, so was Israel ... and just as the tree withered, so Israel will also cease to be the centerpiece for what God is doing on behalf of the whole world. Bottom line: Jesus has come seeking fruit, and finding none, He announces its doom ... same with the Jewish temple.

Fast-forward two thousand years, and we still hear a similar message being communicated. Many people want to experience growth with God, but what is growth with God if we can't look at our lives from one year to the next and see actual "fruit" that's come from it? What "growth" with God has actually taken place if we treat people—coworkers, roommates, family—in exactly the same way we did ten years ago (with control, competition, judgmentalism, or condescension)? Has any real growth with God ever taken place if we've accumulated more Bible knowledge but still treat and respond to those around us in the same old way?

The disciples, though, are fixated on the miraculous (as I would have been) and respond in good *Tommy Boy* fashion, *"What'd You dooo?"* And though their question is irrelevant at the moment, Jesus responds to it. "Truly I say to you, if you have faith and do not doubt, you will not only do what was done to the fig tree, but even if you say to this mountain, 'Be taken up and cast into the sea,' it will happen. And all things you ask in prayer, believing, you will receive" (Matt. 21:21-22, NAS).

In verse 22, He begins with a phrase that makes a broad generalization up front—"all things you ask." Ask for anything and everything, whatever it may be. The sky's the limit. But a limitation is built into the passage—"that you ask *in prayer.*" Another limitation you'll see in other areas of Scripture is when Jesus uses the phrase "in my name." When we pray in Jesus' name, that not only signifies who we are praying through, but also in Jesus we are given a pattern from which we can get a better grasp on how our desires line up with God's desires.

So "that you ask in prayer" provides a context for when your requests are placed in the space of prayer; they immediately begin to look and feel a little different. That is, we have all sorts of desires in different seasons of life, but when those desires are placed in the context of prayer, they immediately take on a different shape. Nevertheless, take all of it to God. Whatever is on your heart and mind that you desire, take those things to God. And in the process of verbalizing those thoughts and wishes to God in the space of prayer, you may end up tossing three-fourths of your requests. Your level of self-awareness might skyrocket as you realize that underneath those requests lies self-promotion or greed. But the things that withstand the test, ask God for those things with all you've got. If you don't believe God can affect the outcomes, then don't pray. Words are vacant without faith.

Listen to how The Message translates Matthew 21:21-22. "But Jesus was matter-of-fact: 'Yes—and if you embrace this kingdom life and don't doubt God, you'll not only do minor feats like I did to the fig tree, but also triumph over huge obstacles. This mountain, for instance, you'll tell, "Go jump in the lake," and it will jump. Absolutely everything, ranging from small to large, as you make it a part of your believing prayer, gets included as you lay hold of God.'"

When rendering a contemporary translation most consistent with the full meaning of the passage, I find it interesting that Eugene Peterson thought it necessary to include this line—"and if you embrace this kingdom life." It seems to reinforce Jesus' words in the Sermon on the Mount, the closest you actually come to hearing anything resembling a recipe or formula from Jesus. "In prayer there is a connection between what God does and what you do. You can't get forgiveness from God, for instance, without also forgiving others. If you refuse to do your part, you cut yourself off from God's part" (Matt. 6:14-15, MSG).

Matthew 6:14-15 sounds like a passage that forbids a compartmentalized understanding of prayer. It's not really possible to absorb the full weight of this passage, then turn around and begin praying without an ounce of action. If you really believe in what it is you're praying about, you'll not only pray about it, you'll also apply elbow grease toward making it happen. Otherwise, there's very little belief in your prayers.

"Believe." Obviously, one of the more foundational terms of the Christian faith. It appears about 140 times throughout the Bible. "The Hebrew and Greek words often translated '***belief***' differ somewhat in meaning from that conveyed by the English verb '***believe***'; they have more the significance of **faith**, understanding, **trust**, constancy, **firm**ness. Hence the Scriptures often appear in our common version to approve and endorse **belief**, when they mean to enforce the necessity of understanding."[4]

In other words, Western Christians understand "believe" to be more cerebral while those in the ancient world understood "believe" much more holistically. Todd Hunter, president of Alpha USA, explains this key difference well:

> Suppose I ask my friend Ben if he "believes" in airplanes.
>
> Ben naturally responds, "Of course I do."
>
> He, then, muffles something derogatory under his breath that I can't completely make out.
>
> Then, pointing in the direction of Sagittarius, he says, "Look, there's one right there flying overhead."
>
> I, then, respond, "Well, have you ever flown?"
>
> To which Ben replies, "Well, not exactly. Last summer I had bought a ticket. I was standing in the terminal just about to board the plane, but once again, my aviophobia kicked in: nausea, hyperventilation, shakiness. I knew good and well that once I boarded the plane, I'd start feeling claustrophobic and end up flipping out on people. So all to say, No, I've still never flown."
>
> "Then you don't believe in airplanes."[5]

So a better English translation of the biblical word "believe" would be to place the full weight of your life in something. (It kind of makes the age-old arguments about "grace versus works" obsolete, doesn't it?) Not just words. Words *and* Action.

Take whatever it is you're praying about, whatever it is you're believing. Then apply movement. Perspiration. Muscle. Initiative. Exertion. Arms working. Feet running. Eyes reading. Mind thinking. Anything less is not a whole-life following of Christ.

VOODOO CHRISTIANITY

You may say, "Hold up there. But isn't there a string of words or an amount of faith—eight ounces, two liters, a quart—that will yield exactly what I want (a successful business venture, a spouse, a car, a new guitar)? I do X, and the machine, err God, does Y?" In the case of this passage in Matthew 21, do you not have the ability—with the right amount of faith—to move mountains? Many, many religious people believe so.

In the early '90s I attended a church that espoused what a friend of mine now calls "Voodoo Christianity." I could be wrong, but I'm fairly certain those belonging to this movement wouldn't call it that, exactly—something about holding the terms "Voodoo" and "Christianity" in the same breath probably wouldn't sit too well. The more well-known term for this movement would be "Positive Confession" or "Word-Faith" (or the slang "Name It and Claim It" or "Confess It and Possess It"). However, my participation in this particular church actually came at a good time in my spiritual journey.

Up through high school, I was fortunate to have been raised in a church setting where many of my leaders and mentors embodied a genuine faith and love for those of us in junior high and high school. A healthy balance between solid structure and caring, humorous leaders proved to be indispensable in those years. But my next church experience provided a certain level of intensity that I'd never known. If I had any questions as to whether Jesus was alive and kicking, they were certainly answered there. The Holy Spirit was defined, described, discussed, and prayed to more than I'd ever heard.

One of the most attractive aspects that it brought to the table had to do with mysticism, an aspect of my faith that I've grown to cherish over the past several years. Those pesky passages in 1 Corinthians with all their mysteries, the occasions where Jesus cast out demons and God spoke in visions, and the times when the early church spoke in tongues—who can turn a blind eye and say those things didn't happen?

In fact, I'd take it a step further. Who has not seen an ill loved one experience a miraculous recovery? Or who hasn't experienced a dream in recent years that was so real you lay there for a few moments trying to tell the difference between reality and dream? Or what about when you just happened to intersect with an old friend, and the timing of your encounter could not have been more perfect? Or when a specific word was spoken that could not have been more relevant to your predicament? Undoubtedly, events take place in our lives that reveal the limitations of science and empiricism. And it was in that particular church that the mystical aspect of my faith began to really take shape.

However, clouds began brewing overhead during my final year. In truth, it took two years before I slowly realized how stunted my perspective had actually become. Outwardly, I talked to other Christians as though we were all human, each with our own issues, all in the same boat. But inwardly I pegged everyone I came in contact with on a spiritual totem pole. It had taken me a while to realize how many under-the-breath comments among church members had created a pressure cooker of spiritual hierarchy. Nonstop judgmentalism. Who's prayed more? Who's attended more Bible studies? Who's spoken in tongues? Who's evangelized the most? Who's given up more things?

Moreover, the mystical aspect of my faith had been left unchecked—a common characteristic of the Positive Confession/

Word-Faith movement. After understanding its roots, I began to see why I was so drawn to this experience. To be precise, the Positive Confession movement is a hybrid system, a blend of mysticism and Gnosticism.[6] In retrospect, the mystical aspect drew me in while the Gnostic elements warped my relationships and understanding of God and self.

As the name Positive Confession/Word-Faith implies, this movement teaches that faith is a matter of what we say more than whom we trust or what truths we embrace and affirm in our hearts. The term "Positive Confession" refers to the teaching that words have creative power. Word-Faith teachers claim that what you say determines everything that happens to you. Your "confessions" (the things you say, especially the things you ask of God) must all be stated positively and without wavering. Then God is required to answer. Bottom line: With enough faith, your words can alter reality.

There are many peculiar ideas and practices in the Word-Faith theology, but what really sets it apart from much of mainstream Christianity is the shift of power, where God must dance to man's attempts to manipulate the spiritual laws of the universe. In my opinion, it's the same song, eighteenth verse. Think: fundamental problem in the story of the Garden of Eden.

The Name It and Claim It movement asserts that God created human beings in His class as "little gods." They espouse that, before the fall, humans had the potential to exercise a "God kind of faith" and could call things into existence. Humans took on Satan's nature by rebelling against God in the Garden of Eden, thus losing the ability to call things into existence. In order to correct this situation, Jesus Christ became a man, died spiritually (taking Satan's nature upon Himself), went to hell, was "born again," and rose from the dead with God's nature. After this, Jesus sent the Holy Spirit to duplicate the Incarnation in believers so they might fulfill their calling to be little gods.

It follows, then, that those who have had the Incarnation duplicated in them by the Holy Spirit (thus giving them the ability to exercise the "God kind of faith") should be successful in every area of their lives. Furthermore, hardships like indebtedness, illness, and even being left by one's spouse show lack of faith because these problems should be eliminated by "claiming" God's promises.

An actual story:

> A pastor and his wife have three daughters. Two of the three were described as very feminine girls while the third was regarded for much of her early years as a tomboy. When the third daughter found herself in the middle of her high school years, her father, the pastor, asked her to come up on stage one Sunday during a church service. She hesitantly moved forward toward the stage as her father began retelling an account that happened sixteen years prior ...
>
> When his wife was pregnant with their third daughter, a woman in the church approached the wife one Sunday "prophesying" that they'd have a boy. From the father's perspective, she "spoke it into motion," something he certainly couldn't "reverse." So from the moment she was born, he began relating to her more like a boy than a girl.
>
> Sixteen years later, he's calling her up to the stage, and he's aiming to "reverse" the supernatural events that had been "spoken into motion" so many years before. In his own way, he was repenting of the way he treated his daughter for so many years.

Imagine how humiliated this girl had to be!

For you and me, red flags should be raised when we come across religious people who elevate themselves to positions of equality with God. Many people talk as though they've figured out how to force God's hand. They've apparently broken the code. At times the language can be thoroughly spiritual, but the intent is clear. A shift in power has taken place. The apostle Paul battled against this frequently in the days of the early church. In fact, Gnosticism was specifically one of the major first-century teachings Paul fought against in several of the later letters (Colossians, 1 Timothy, 2 Timothy, Titus).

At some point, all of us must come to grips with this central question: "Can you ever know *for certain*—with 100 percent verifiable proof—which prayers pass the test and will get answered and which don't?" No. You cannot. There's only one God. Leave certainty to the field of mathematics and the laws of physics. Incorporate trust in the field of prayer. All we can do is strive to unload as many of the nonsense prayer requests that have no business being offered, and of the things you desire that "pass the test," pray with everything you've got about those things.

At my house every single day, a severe storm of one sort or another hits. I'm not sure which—tornado, typhoon, cyclone, or hurricane. I hear all of these storms are very similar animals and just depend on location. Tornadoes hit more inland while hurricanes stay at sea. Hurricanes hit in the Atlantic, but everywhere else in the world, they're considered typhoons. And tornadoes are usually smaller in size than hurricanes. So it seems there are some days when the path of destruction left at our house at 8:30 p.m. resembles tornadic activity, and other days a hurricane.

Let's suppose it's Thursday night, and Jen and I have just gotten our kids to bed. The destruction left in the wake of the day was *definitely* of hurricane proportions. Wooden Thomas the Train railroad tracks, a couple of Barbies, some Dr. Seuss literature, and a few balls have been strewn from here to there in no particular pattern. Jen is organizing some things in the living room while I'm lying on the couch watching TV.

Fortunately, we've been married long enough for me to have picked up on two or three things. Like, I surrendered on the toilet seat battle midway through year one. It was the middle of the night, completely dark throughout the house, she walked into the bathroom at 2:00 a.m. and fell through. All right, all right, I'll put the seat down. After a few years of marriage, I also decided to give her the benefit of the doubt and say she wasn't "faking strep throat" after watching her sweat bullets beneath nine layers of blankets, glands the size of Frankenstein, and some sort of white crap on her tonsils. I guess I've picked up on a few things over time.

So it's Thursday night, the hurricane has hit, and Jen is preparing the kids' lunches for Mother's Day Out. Something deep within tells me not to position my slouch toward the kitchen and say, "Hey, Jen ... Do—You—Want—Me—To—Pick—Up—These—Toys?" Because the chances are incredibly high that some sort of snappy response will be shot back in my direction, "Oh, no, you keep on lying there. I was hoping to do that myself after I'm finished with these lunches, hanging their clothes, and paying the bills." Good call. Probably wouldn't be an appropriate question.

There are many things I don't have to ask her opinion on, and the reason is because I already know it. That is, marriage is a way of life shared by two people where conversation is almost unceasing. And when it comes to prayer, this is the best hope we have in determining which things are a waste of breath and which are legit. That prayer will become a way of life.

UNLOADING CERTAINTY, EMBRACING MYSTERY

In today's postmodern culture, we've been reminded of this beautiful truth that we humans are an experience-oriented bunch. We are deeply affected by a canon by Bach, a thick steak, a well-crafted film, a blooming daffodil, freshly brewed coffee. We are each intricately designed with an intellect and emotions, a sense of smell, taste, and touch.

The modern era tried to convince us that we could detach our brains from our bodies and study a thing apart from our hearts, history, and senses, but the postmodern era has exposed that fallacy. We can't be reduced to a single organ, like the brain. We're much, much more than that.

Recently one morning, my four-year-old daughter walked into our bathroom as Jen and I were brushing our teeth. She stepped into the small, connected toilet room and pulled out the scale that was laid against the wall. Avery laid it on the floor behind me in the middle of the bathroom and, before even stepping on the scale, announced she was now "up to sixty pounds!"

She jumped on, and a few seconds later it registered thirty-eight. Pulling herself up off the floor, she asked, "What does it say, Daddy?" I threw up a high-five, and in my I'm-selling-a-Lexus voice said, "THIRTY-EIGHT!" Didn't matter one iota. She drooped her head dejectedly in utter disappointment. Now, how often does this happen? I should've caught this on video to replay when she's sixteen just so I could say, "There was a time when ..."

I stepped inside my closet, grabbed a pair of jeans, and turned around, and Avery's entire body, from head to toe, was prostrate on the carpet in a flying Superman position with only her stomach on the scale. Immediately, I was thinking, *Now this is gonna be good.* Naturally, I said, "What are you doing?" And she responded in a tone as if I'd forgotten the alphabet. "I'm weighing my bel-ly!"—Silly me. How could I not have known?

Try as we may, we can't measure a human individual piece by piece. An arm here, a leg there, brains over here, feet over there. In every experience of life, we bring our whole selves to the table. Not just our brains and not just our hearts. All of it. However, many people through the years have not acknowledged this truth, supposing they could understand God completely with 100 percent intellectual coherency, 100 percent certainty. Only after all of the dots were connected cognitively would they begin following Him.

In my experience, it doesn't seem as though that's the way it works. In fact, Jesus seemed to intertwine loving God with loving others. "Jesus said, 'Love the Lord your God with all your passion and prayer and intelligence. This is the most important, the first on any list. But there is a second to set alongside it: Love others as well as you love yourself. These two commands are pegs; everything in God's Law and the Prophets hangs from them'" (Matt. 22:37-40, MSG).

In other words, there seems to be different kinds of knowing. There is a kind of knowing that comes from the shoulders up, and this kind of knowing is indispensable. God is the sole creator of our brains, correct? Certain Christians de-emphasize this aspect of creation as much as possible, treating the human brain as though it were the spawn of Satan. Other Christians, though, treat the human brain as though it were the sole proprietor of truth, as though it held the monopoly on knowledge.

But there is another kind of knowing that incorporates the whole life, not just the brain, and this kind of knowing is also indispensable but doesn't receive near the merit that it should.

There is a kind of knowing that comes from living in the Way of Christ, and somewhere along the way—*in the living*—I discover for myself that Jesus is right and true.

The apostle Paul alluded to this fact when saying, "For now we see in a mirror, dimly, but then we will see face to face. Now I know only *in part*; then I will know fully, even as I have been fully known" (1 Cor. 13:12, NRSV, emphasis mine). In fact, what if certainty has never been part of God's desire for our lives? Because 100 percent certainty with anything in life—finances, job security, illness, the future—would create the illusion that we don't really need God after all.

So much of the Christian faith isn't solidified in closure, perfect clarity, and bow-tied events. If in doubt, try explaining the Trinity to a five-year-old. At times, it seems the Christian faith is shrouded in mystery, ambiguity, and paradox—apparent contradictions. For instance, the Christian faith seems to rest on this recipe: You do A, and God doesn't do B, He does Z. You screw up, and God extends to you His love. Grace. It doesn't produce an ounce of logical sense. It doesn't jive with the natural laws of gravity. But Christians believe it to be real.

Or try this paradox: Do whatever you want to do and experience an unseen but very real sort of slavery. Most people today believe that doing whatever one wants to do equals freedom. I can tell you, though, that I am perfectly free to eat whatever the heck I want to eat, but an unbridled, unseen force of cosmic proportions just had me downing a Nutty Chocolate-Chipper Cookie at Panera Bread. I am free to eat whatever I choose, but I swear to you it doesn't feel like uninhibited freedom. I don't feel all that liberated. Not just in eating. A number of things could fill the blank where we apparently have all the freedom in the world to do as we please, but it's not that easy. The apostle Paul articulated this well.

> What I don't understand about myself is that I decide one way, but then I act another, doing things I absolutely despise. So if I can't be trusted to figure out what is best for myself and then do it, it becomes obvious that God's command is necessary. But I need something more! For if I know the law but still can't keep it, and if the power of sin within me keeps sabotaging my best intentions, I obviously need help! I realize that I don't have what it takes. I can will it, but I can't do it. I decide to do good, but I don't really do it; I decide not to do bad, but then I do it anyway. My decisions, such as they are, don't result in actions. Something has gone wrong deep within me and gets the better of me every time. It happens so regularly that it's predictable. The moment I decide to do good, sin is there to trip me up. I truly delight in God's commands, but it's pretty obvious that not all of me joins in that delight. Parts of me covertly rebel, and just when I least expect it, they take charge. I've tried everything and nothing helps. I'm at the end of my rope. Is there no one who can do anything for me? Isn't that the real question? The answer, thank God, is that Jesus Christ can and does. He acted to set things right in this life of contradictions where I want to serve God with all my heart and mind, but am pulled by the influence of sin to do something totally different. (Rom. 7:15-25, MSG)

Evidently, written into the DNA of the universe are mysteries and paradox that surpass the human intellect but reach the depths of the soul. It is good to be reminded that we have been created with such intricacy. That we are much more than mathematical equations or little boxes of circuitry. That there is depth and design to who we are. For all that God is and all that God offers, we must respond likewise—not just from the shoulders up, but with our whole lives.

8

CHAPTER

THE EASTERN WAY

I don't know when exactly it happened, but somewhere along the way, my communication with God outgrew all that was contained in the word "prayer." It sounds a bit ridiculous, but in my former days, my understanding of prayer could best be defined as follows:

> When air is forced up the trachea from the lungs at a certain pressure, it is able to force its way through the vocal cords, pushing them open. As air passes through the glottis, the air pressure in the glottis falls. Because of the drop in pressure, the vocal cords snap together, at the lower edge first, closing again. The cycle then begins again. A single cycle of opening and closing takes in the region of 1/100th second: therefore, the cycle repeats at rates in the region of one hundred times per second (to be more specific, between about eighty to two hundred cycles per second). This rate is too rapid for the human ear to be able to discriminate each individual opening/closing of the vocal cords. However,

> we perceive variations in the overall rate of vibration as changes in the pitch of the voice, "pitch" being the perceptual correlate of acoustic frequency.

Naturally, when these openings and closings of the vocal cords push out an acoustic frequency that addresses the Supreme Being, you have prayer. So you could very well ask,

"Kyle, have you prayed today?"
"How much have you prayed?"
"When did you pray?"
"How long did you pray?"

To give it an even more convicting punch, you could number your questions. Like, "*Number one*: Kyle, have you prayed today? *Number two*: How much have you prayed?"

And I could respond, "Yes.Thismorningat7:30am,airwasforced-upthetracheathroughthelungsatacertainpressurethatforceditsway-throughthevocalchordspushingthemopenandclosed,openand-closed,openandclosed, atafrequencytoorapidforthehumanearto-discriminateeachindividualopeningandclosingofthecordsand-creatinganacousticfrequencydirectedtowardGod,so,toansweryourquestion,yes,thismorning,thisopeningandclosingofthevocal-chordshappenedforadurationofsixminutesandforty-oneseconds. I'mtryingtogetituptoeight,butIhaven'tgottenthereyet."

Somewhere along my journey, though, this definition of prayer became too constrictive, too narrow, not big enough to fully contain my communication with God. It was sufficient for my younger days in youth group but not wide enough to capture the full scope of what was taking place with God.

As life with God grows, expands, deepens, and becomes more whole, we are forced to begin thinking outside of the box. It feels a bit pathetic to admit that for most of my life I've approached prayer within the framework of "what counts" and "what doesn't count." Pathetic, but realistic nonetheless.

THE PRESENCE OF GOD

Why is it when we begin talking about "THE PRESENCE OF GOD" (insert creepy, ghoulish voice), we suddenly find ourselves at a Benny Hinn Crusade or exorcising Ouija boards? The feel of the conversation shifts in the direction of vague superstition, like we're talking about black cats, ladders, and knocking on wood.

I realize we're talking about a subject matter that's obviously unscientific, so it's not going to feel like a lecture on molecular DNA. However, just because this subject matter employs other methods of knowing—intuition, historical observation, the senses—it shouldn't be exempt from intelligible discussion. Many of us have had experiences that we'd say were more supernatural in nature, where our language at times seems impotent. However, that doesn't mean the basis of our belief is "blind faith." For anyone interested in consistent, nourished growth with God, "blind faith" should not be the bedrock of the relationship. Periodic supernatural experiences, though incredibly affirming, should not provide the life blood of relationship with God. The constant searching out of spiritual fireworks is not indicative of a person full of faith but a person in constant need of more reinforcement. The more mature learners of Christ take very seriously what it means to live out friendship with God in the details, in the mundane.

Now, I feel as though I need to give some level of warning here. What I'm needing to do over these next few pages is to perform one of my Jedi mind tricks on you. Don't worry, it's not illegal. It's not a mind *trip*. I said, mind *trick*. I'll admit that once

I've wielded the force, it will help to situate the next few pages if you've got a light saber or, in the very least, a few combat moves. Allow me to explain ...

> **OB1** (me): These next few pages are pure gold.
> Trooper (you): These next few pages are pure gold.
> **OB1** (me): You will accept everything that's been submitted.
> Trooper (you): I will accept everything that's been submitted.

Nothing has shaped my understanding of the Christian faith more radically in recent years than finding out how thoroughly Western I am. When I say "Western," I'm not talking about Roy Rogers. I'm not talking about whether or not I can saddle a horse or how fast I can holster a gun. I'm talking geography. I'm talking about the fact that the historical Christian faith did not originate in Topeka, Kansas. I'm talking about the fact that the Christian faith has its roots in the East—the Middle East to be exact—where people held (and still hold) vastly different world-views and assumptions about God, relationships, and reality. They even had different assumptions about the air we breathe ...

Surprisingly, Jews in the first century didn't imagine heaven as we do today. They didn't conceive of a distant faraway land involving blue skies, puffy white clouds, and streets of gold. In the Old Testament, "heaven" or "the heavens" (plural) was not a distant place but the direct presence of God.[1]

One Old Testament story finds Hagar, Abraham's concubine, in the desert with her child dying of thirst. She couldn't stand to watch her child die. She was on the brink of doing something tragic—placing him out of her sight by leaving him—when this happens:

> Meanwhile, God heard the boy crying. The angel of God called from Heaven to Hagar, "What's wrong,

> Hagar? Don't be afraid. God has heard the boy and knows the fix he's in. Up now; go get the boy. Hold him tight. I'm going to make of him a great nation." Just then God opened her eyes. She looked. She saw a well of water. She went to it and filled her canteen and gave the boy a long, cool drink. (Gen. 21:17-19, MSG)

In the next chapter, Genesis 22, Abraham was inches away from sacrificing Isaac when this happens:

> Just then an angel of God called to him out of Heaven, "Abraham! Abraham!" ... The angel of God spoke from Heaven a second time to Abraham: "I swear—God's sure word!—because you have gone through with this, and have not refused to give me your son, your dear, dear son, I'll bless you—oh, how I'll bless you! And I'll make sure that your children flourish—like stars in the sky! like sand on the beaches! And your descendants will defeat their enemies. All nations on Earth will find themselves blessed through your descendants because you obeyed me." (Gen. 22:11, 15-18, MSG)

In both cases, God or an angel calls "out of heaven," but "heaven" is never considered to be somewhere out beyond the clouds or by the moon. Instead, "heaven" is understood to be "at hand"—literally, in the air or atmosphere surrounding our bodies.[2]

Acts 11 provides some of the same language, although Dallas Willard considers many translations downright embarrassing. Willard explains that in a span of five verses, we find the same Greek phrase, *tou ouranou*, used three different times but translated in different ways.

> I was in the city of Joppa praying, and in a trance I saw a vision. There was something like a large sheet coming down from heaven (*tou ouranou*), being lowered by its four corners; and it came close to me. As I looked at it closely I saw four-footed animals, beasts of prey, reptiles, and birds of the air (*tou ouranou*). I also heard a voice saying to me, "Get up, Peter; kill and eat." But I replied, "By no means, Lord; for nothing profane or unclean has ever entered my mouth." But a second time the voice answered from heaven (*tou ouranou*), "What God has made clean, you must not call profane." (Acts 11:5-9, NRSV)

In other words, when we encounter or experience the presence of God, the image we have in the Scriptures is not of a God who exists in a remote location, then rushes to our side at every beck and call. God is not the offensive coordinator of a football team who lives in the great coaches' box in the sky and only periodically intervenes on the field of play when He's requested. Rather, God inhabits the space surrounding our bodies.

Paul reinforces this perspective in Acts 17 while addressing many of the modern-day philosophers on Mars Hill.

> Then Paul stood in front of the Areopagus and said, "Athenians, I see how extremely religious you are in every way. For as I went through the city and looked carefully at the objects of your worship, I found among them an altar with the inscription, 'To an unknown god.' What therefore you worship as unknown, this I proclaim to you. The God who made the world and everything in it, he who is Lord of heaven and earth, does not live in shrines made by human hands, nor is he served by human hands, as though he needed anything, since he himself gives to all mortals life and breath and

all things. From one ancestor he made all nations to inhabit the whole earth, and he allotted the times of their existence and the boundaries of the places where they would live, so that they would search for God and perhaps grope for him and find him—though indeed he is not far from each one of us. For 'In him we live and move and have our being'; as even some of your own poets have said, 'For we too are his offspring.'" (Acts 17:22-28, NRSV)

Now, here's where things get interesting. For Paul, he is not speaking abstractly or theoretically. One author says that Paul is speaking in the most literal way possible, a fact that all Jews were aware of, "that they would seek God, if perhaps they might grope for Him and find Him, though He is not far from each one of us; for in Him we live and move and exist."

"In Him, we live and move and have our being"—a fact that Paul believed quite literally. Here's where the Scriptures find whatever edge of absurdity we're standing on and push us off. Paul even proceeds to name this space in which we "live and move and have our being" in a later New Testament letter: "He is the image of the invisible God, the firstborn of all creation; for *in him all things in heaven and on earth were created, things visible and invisible*, whether thrones or dominions or rulers or powers—all things have been created through him and for him. He himself is before all things, *and in him all things hold together*" (Col. 1:15-17, NRSV, emphasis mine).

Are you familiar with who this passage in Colossians is referring to as "He"? Are you catching this?

To consider such things makes me feel as though I'm in the control room at NASA charting space travel or something. What a mind-blowing thought! Chalk up another title to the long, long list of titles attributed to Jesus. Now we have: Jesus—The "Glue of the universe."[3] In some sort of beyond-mental-comprehension way (or at least, my mental comprehension), Jesus holds the universe in place yet remains intimately present with us.

In light of Jesus' constant presence, it shows just how ridiculous some statements truly are. Statements like "God just *showed up*." Have you ever heard this statement or said it yourself? How could this truly be? If God has literally infused His presence in the atmosphere surrounding our bodies, then the one who "just showed up" is who, exactly? The central issue, now, is no longer an issue of God's presence but our awareness.[4]

And this has tremendous implications for the way we understand prayer! Previously, prayer was defined in terms of quantity and duration. Now, prayer has become more fluid and open-ended, lacking compartments or parameters. Paul puts it this way in Romans 12:1: "So here's what I want you to do, God helping you: Take your everyday, ordinary life—your sleeping, eating, going-to-work, and walking-around life—and place it before God as an offering. Embracing what God does for you is the best thing you can do for him" (MSG).

For this reason and more, we can take a step back and define prayer. Finally, at last! A definition we can all embrace that's large enough to contain the full scope of our lives. Luis of Granada, a sixteenth-century Christian spiritual writer, simply defined it as "any raising of the heart to God."[5] Any raising of the heart to God ...

> at school, before you eat, while you drive, in the locker room, at home, eyes open, eyes shut, before an exam, through the woods, feeding the dog, on the deck, walking to class, in the morning, before you sleep, won-

> dering about the world, after the fight, looking for an answer, because you care, because you don't care, flying across the ocean, on your knees, to erase or to remember, when you're happy, when you're scared, when no one else hears, using ancient ideas or new ones, singing or screaming, writing a letter, in a journal, at the interview, with or without something to say, to get real, on the date, sacred or irreverent, help! help! help!, loud or soft, at work, floating or sinking, after you fail, after you succeed, hands folded or raised to the sky, with a friend, with your dad, for your friends, for your family, during the game, at the meet, to find Jesus, on the mountaintop, in the valley, when you feel alive, when you feel half-dead, under attack, or to attack, to reorganize, at the concert, for composure, to praise, to worship, to just listen, wherever, whenever, however ...[6]

That's prayer. Redefined. Or, to be precise, *historically* defined. And my guess is that it's already been going on in your life. It's just that no one has ever said anything about it being legit, about it *counting*. So may I be the first to come along and tell you that the persistent, silent awareness of God that threads through your day, even in the most mundane times—on a bike, in a journal, after the movie, in the car—they all count. Not only do they count, but that fluid, seamless life with God you exhibit has actually been God's hope all along.

In the 1600s Brother Lawrence experienced this at a profoundly deep level. In *The Practice of the Presence of God*, he says,

> I make it my business to persevere in His holy presence, wherein I keep myself by a simple attention and a general fond regard to God, which I may call an ACTUAL PRESENCE of God; or, to speak better, an habitual, silent, and secret conversation of the soul with God,

> which often causes me joys and raptures inwardly, and sometimes also outwardly, so great that I am forced to use means to moderate them and prevent their appearance to others.[7]

A SECRET CONVERSATION OF THE SOUL

Kathleen Norris describes this well. In her book, *The Cloister Walk*, she recounts what Sunday morning worship services look like in one small town. She says, "At the worship services of Hope and Spencer, there's a time after the sermon, and before the Lord's Prayer, in which people are asked to speak of any particular joys they wish to share with the congregation,"[8] or concerns they want the congregation to address in communal prayer during the service and throughout the upcoming week. Norris says that it's a vital part of the worship, an opportunity to discover things you didn't know: "that the young woman sitting in the pew in front of you is desperately worried about her gravely ill brother in Oregon, that the widower in his eighties sitting across the aisle is overjoyed at the birth of his first great-grandchild."[9]

"Our worship sometimes goes into a kind of suspended animation, as people speak in great detail about the medical condition of their friends or relatives. We wince; we squirm; we sigh; and it's good for us."[10] Moments like this are when the congregation is reminded that listening is "often the major part of ministry, that people in a crisis need to tell their story, from beginning to end, and the best thing—often the only thing—that you can do is to sit there and take it in."[11]

Norris goes on to say that these moments are the core of our worship. "What I think of as the vertical dimension of Presbyterian worship—the hymns in exalted language that bolster our faith, the Bible readings, the sermon that may help us through the coming week—finds a strong (and necessary) compliment in the localized, horizontal dimension of these simple statements of 'joys and concerns.'"[12]

This aspect of the service has, for many years, also been strongly ecumenical.

> Not long ago, the congregation learned from one of his longtime friends that Bill O'Rourke had died. (Wild Bill to his friends way back in his drinking days.) Most of us knew that he'd been failing in the Veterans Hospital in Sturgis for some time. I knew him casually, but missed him. An old-time cowboy—he broke horses for the U.S. Cavalry between the world wars—he was permanently bow-legged. In retirement he'd become a fixture at the café on Main Street; you could nearly always find him there, holding court. More rarely, I'd run into him outside. Bill would wait for someone to come by who would stop and admire one of the Ford pickup trucks from the early 1950s that he kept polished and in running condition. When his death was announced, a sigh ran through the congregation. All but the youngest members and our pastor had known him for years and had their own Wild Bill stories.
>
> It was an odd moment. Bill's death felt like a loss to me, to many people, but we also knew that our young minister would know nothing of him. The pastor was about to begin the intercessory prayer that follows this part of worship, when one of Bill's oldest friends couldn't resist saying, "You know, Bill paid me the first fifty cents I ever made, back in 1930." The minister smiled but looked a bit nonplussed. He took a breath as if to start the prayer. From a pew in the back of the church came a voice, "And I'll bet you still have it."

> Of course we laughed for a good long time before continuing with our worship; it was the kind of story Bill would have enjoyed. He didn't care much for church decorum, but he took some aspects of religion seriously enough. The last time I saw him was at the Lutheran church where he'd come for the funeral of an old friend. Bill sat alone at the back of the church. "I wanted to make sure they gave him a good sendoff," is all he said to me after the service. He was apparently satisfied.
>
> When the minister finally got to say his "Let us pray," we were ready. We had been praying all along. We had been ourselves before God.[13]

We had been praying all along. We had been ourselves before God.

Henri Nouwen said that when prayer becomes a way of life for you, it does not mean that you think about God *in contrast* to thinking about other things, or that you spend time with God *instead of* spending time with other people. Rather, it means to think and live in the presence of God. As soon as we begin to divide our thoughts into thoughts about God and thoughts about people and events, we remove God from our daily life and put Him in a pious little niche where we can think pious thoughts and experience pious feelings.[14] Our instruction in 1 Thessalonians 5, "pray without ceasing," then finds new meaning.

9
CHAPTER
PRAYER AS A WAY OF LIFE?

Recently, it became apparent to me that we were missing the boat—that our approach to God and faith had become far too quantifiable and compartmentalized. In the same week, I had virtually the same conversation with two different people in our church. Both communicated similar things about the status of their relationships with God.

When I sat down with each of them individually for coffee, both explained that they felt their spiritual lives had made very little headway in the past several months. I, then, started probing, asking questions, and it wasn't long before I found out that for both of them, their prayer lives had become this beautiful, fluid, open-ended conversation with God that affected most of their actual day. At this point, I started scratching my head ...

So I kept probing, asking more and more questions, and I found that as they looked back over their past year, they felt they had really made some strides in a number of areas: they were approaching relationships with friends and family in a more healthy manner; they were approaching their finances more responsibly than they had in years past; and a few extra steps had been taken in discovering who they were and where they were headed in life.

Now, I was *really* scratching my head, wondering if I had heard them right: "Okay, earlier. Remember *earlier?* Remember when you said that you felt as though your spiritual life had fallen off the map? That you haven't experienced growth in the past year? Is it possible you came in here high, and the drugs have just now worn off? I don't understand."

As we dug further, this is what we found out: both individuals grew up in a church youth group setting where the annual spiritual cycle went like this ...

> Summer youth camp = spiritual high, Scripture reading goes up, amount of prayer goes up, emotional intensity goes up ... and this carries them into the first part of the school year.
>
> October, November, December = spiritually dry, emotionally down, Scripture reading down, prayer life down.
>
> Youth group winter retreat = spiritual high, emotional intensity high, Scripture reading goes up, amount of prayer goes up.
>
> March, April, May = spiritual low, low emotional intensity, Scripture reading down, amount of prayer down.

In other words, their understanding of spiritual growth had become quantifiable. It was solely attached to their level of emotional intensity, amount of Scripture reading, and amount of prayer. Forget the possibility that they were still being formed in the way of Christ.

But when they left high school, they actually became more constant. Less roller-coaster. They enjoyed more steady, consistent, sustained growth. Until one day, they turned around and realized their prayer life had become more fluid and open-ended—and they didn't have a category for that. So they just said, "Nothing is happening with God." The only categories they had involved the number of Scripture verses read and the amount of time spent in isolated prayer. It seems the Pharisee legacy has been passed on.

Are Scripture reading and intentional times of prayer vital to spiritual growth? Absolutely. But if those moments breed a compartmentalized life that pays little attention to the whole life, then something is amiss. Prayer must become a way of life. But how exactly does that happen? How does prayer become "a way of life"? Unload the pleasantries, the lovely spiritual descriptions that sound good on paper, and let's get down to the nitty-gritty. I have no use for ambiguous phrases that don't translate into real life. And apparently, neither does Holly, a girl in our church who was experiencing dissatisfaction in the way she approached God and prayer.

Recently, in our community of faith, we held conversations about this very subject. Afterward, I received an email from Holly. Our email discussion led us down the road of understanding the meaning of everyday phrases like "deep connection with God." Eventually, we began talking through what it looks like to experience God in the mundane details of life—what it looks like for prayer to become "a way of life."

----- Original Message -----
Sent: Tuesday, March 01, 2005 11:58 PM
Subject: dear kyle

Kyle,
hey there...
I feel silly writing you. I am not completely sure why, but every time I have wanted to email you, I haven't. So this time I am going for it. I have a difficult time articulating, so I hope that this doesn't confuse you.

The discussions of prayer lately have got me thinking about my prayer life. It has basically been non-existent for several months now. I can't remember a time in my life that i have been "super-prayerful." All of these things that you have said about prayer, such as make it conversational and not to have it too formal, are how i was taught to pray. It seems to be a fresh thing for some people that may help them take a new look on prayer, but for me it is normal. I think that because i became a Christian when i was twelve, i jumped in around the time when kids were getting to their questioning stages and this began being taught. I never was the kid who thought that I had to "go through the motions." this seems to be a relatively new idea to everyone else, but i never had what came before. I never thought that you HAD to do your quiet time or that i had to do this and that to be a good Christian the way other kids did. I feel like I missed out on a step... the "hardcore step" if you will. (this may be some assumption that i am making that isn't true). Many people say that they are feeling further from God. I feel as though I have never really made it up to a really high/close point to have fallen back from.

So basically, i am thinking that people are changing their thoughts on prayer and that is helping them. Meanwhile, I am praying the same "way" they are and feel no result. I too, just as the girl you quoted two weeks ago, feel as though I am talking to the air. I feel this is my fault, that if i truly wanted to hear God or seek Him, that I would be seeing, hearing, feeling Him. I seem to know many things and I know the churchy answers for things, but I don't truly feel them and live them out.

That is a little rocky and jumps subjects a bit, but it will have to do. Sorry about that. I really hope that i didn't confuse you. And I don't really have a question, I just keep thinking that something must be done and I can't seem to figure out, alone, what that is. Thanks for your time and for reading this.

~Holly

Sent: Wednesday, March 02, 2005 11:22 AM
Subject: Re: dear kyle

Hey Holly

Thanks for sharing this. I think it really made a lot of sense to me, actually, and has left me wondering more. For instance, it made a lot of sense when you said that you feel you never really hit a "high point/close point" to fall back from...and that "going through the motions" was never really a problem for you. But it sounded like you were inferring that you've never felt a level of deep connection with God in the first place. So first, is that what you're saying?

And then second, how would you describe "a deep connection with God"? Do you have an idea or feel of what that would look like/entail? Maybe one analogy would be, what makes you feel you have a deeper connection with some friends as opposed to others?

Kyle

----- Original Message -----
Sent: Thursday, March 03, 2005 1:08 AM
Subject: RE: dear kyle

Kyle,
I think that you are right about me not really having a deep connection with God. I am not going to say that i have never felt this, but if/when I have, it didn't last long. Perhaps this is why i haven't "gone through the motions," or maybe that is why these experiences didn't last long. Describing what i think is a deep connection with God is difficult. I have ideas but not words. Let's see, I think this would entail being in constant (or close to constant) prayer and getting some response. (i do feel as though i have experienced this before). I also think that it would be a strong feeling of His presence. Of course reading the Bible is a huge part of this and sometimes i am thinking "if i begin reading more often, then maybe i will feel Him more," and other times i am thinking "prayer first, then the Bible." I haven't figured out anything that seems to work well and at the same time i am thinking that i don't want to have to have some book or anyone tell me how to do this. I feel like i could figure out the first steps alone. Kind of frustrating. i am stopping here b/c it is bed time. goodnight or rather, good morning.

~Holly

Sent: Thursday, March 3, 2005 10:42 AM
Subject: Re: dear kyle

Hey—when I asked those questions, they really weren't loaded. I wasn't insinuating anything. They were honest questions—because that's what I'm trying to get to the heart of...how do you describe "deep connection with God"? Or maybe an even better way of putting it is, how do you develop a deep "abiding" in God (sorry if that word sounds a bit too spiritual)? But I think that would be our goal—not for us to develop a bunch of little moments here and there where we experience pious thoughts and pious feelings and voice pious words. Surely, God must want more out of us than brief moments of piety, right? And yet experiences of delving into scripture or isolated prayer are DEFINITELY part of it but not all of it.

For instance...when you go to Dallas to listen to those bands, what is your experience like? Is that a purely secular aspect of your life that doesn't have a thing to do with God? Honestly, what's going on there in your heart/mind/soul when you're experiencing the beauty and energy of that thing?

Kyle

p.s. I think Dave NAILS all of this in the first forty pages of *Praise Habit*...not to send you to more reading but I'm definitely encouraging you to think outside of the box here and actually apply "spiritual" labels to many spiritual things that are already taking place in your life (although I think perhaps very few people have ever come along and told you that). Maybe in our next exchange you can walk me through your typical day and detail for me what is secular and what is sacred about it...even the minutia.

----- Original Message -----
Sent: Friday, March 04, 2005 12:55 AM
Subject: RE: dear kyle

ok i get what you are saying. i realize that scripture reading and prayer are not the only things for us to do and the only times we will experience God. Like you said, when i go to hear bands play, these are some of the greatest times. Music is a huge part of my life and I see God throughout lyrics and melodies, etc.

hmm ok my typical day...
~waking up (at the very last possible moment)...
~deciding whether or not to drive or walk to class...when i walk, i have my ipod and sometimes i am thinking yay for this song and other times i am thinking...maybe i should just be quiet and spend my walk thinking/praying...
~class—blah blah, i really don't like school much...of course thoughts are different from class to class...for example: in my spanish class, i am praying for understanding...i truly dislike spanish, but that is b/c i don't make good grades in that class and it is difficult...then there is brit lit where my professor is the cutest little lady ever...she tells us not only about the literature but how it applies to our lives and how they teach us life lessons...along the way she does the same...her love for Christ radiates off of her...she amazes me...I have thanked God so many times that i get to spend my tuesday/thurs afternoons with her...
~my mind is constantly thinking about the next meal...so lunchtime...trying not to eat too much so that Steph won't think that i am going to get fat...
~work...when i slack at work i think of Charles Swindoll's book *improving your serve*...it makes me think of the times i have worked at younglife camps and worked that much harder b/c i know that i am doing it for God and for the kids...not for pay...i try and carry that over into my silly little job at the Spirit shop...
~during many of my days i make a stop at CG...and chat with pals...common grounds is kind of a getaway...reminds me of the *cheers* theme song "where everybody knows your name, and they're always glad you came"...haha
~then comes dinner...same scenario as lunch..."therefore honor God w/ your body." i try!
~there is always a time that i sit at my computer and waste time by reading online journals...this is super fun...and i make my entries mostly silly, i think i do it for attention really...ha... simply fun
~steph and i normally have a "debriefing" time after class or at

the end of the day...this is always fun and i think this is how we keep our friendship going b/c we know it gets rocky sometimes...
~Meg and i do the same kind of thing...i love that girl!
~i read for class and then read part of a book (on rare occasion i will open up the message at this time)...say my nightly prayers (hopefully i won't fall asleep) and go to bed

kinda random and silly...just like me...haha...
i have read the first part of Dave's book but i am going to go look over it again...it's so funny...

~Holly

p.s. Skate Night was super fun! always a good time...you and Jenn are pretty much amazing sk8ters...ha...

Sent: Friday, March 04, 2005 10:59 AM
Subject: Re: dear kyle

Skate Night was definitely good times.

Thanks for walking through your day like this...my responses are below in italics...
Kyle

hmm ok my typical day...
~waking up (at the very last possible moment)...

I wonder if this might be a good starting place...even waking up five minutes before you typically do could give you a few minutes to lay in bed and voice a prayer or read a brief something—one of the purposes of this is not only to connect with God but also to train your mind to develop a sense of God-awareness for the rest of the day.

~deciding whether or not to drive or walk to class...when i walk, i have my ipod and sometimes i am thinking yay for this song and other times i am thinking...maybe i should just be quiet and spend my walk thinking/praying...

cool—go with your instincts there and what you're feeling that particular day...if you're at a place where you're needing more quiet, that might be a great time...

~class—blah blah, i really don't like school much...of course thoughts are different from class to class...for example: in my spanish class, i am praying for understanding...i truly dislike spanish, but that is b/c i don't make good grades in that class and it is difficult...

This is a healthy rub that you'll most likely have in some form the rest of your life. Yea! That there will always be crap in our lives that demands we just strive to be persistent even though there's not an ounce of appeal to that thing. In technical terms, I'd say we've been created to live our lives in the image of God...and since our God is characterized by perseverance and consistency, there should be aspects of our lives that reflect the same. (Sorry! :>)

then there is brit lit where my professor is the cutest little lady ever...she tells us not only about the literature but how it applies to our lives and how they teach us life lessons...along the way she does the same...her love for Christ radiates off of her...she amazes me...I have thanked God so many times that i get to spend my tuesday/thurs afternoons with her...

EXCELLENT! That's great awareness on your end too!

~my mind is constantly thinking about the next meal...so lunchtime...trying not to eat too much so that Steph won't think that i am going to get fat...

Well said, Holly—and I appreciate your vulnerability here. If you see a pattern of "Steph-voice" affecting your decisions, first become aware of that, then begin exploring why you're giving her so much voice here… I'll bet there is a communal aspect to this where giving her voice in your life is healthy and I'll also bet there is something unhealthy about how much voice you are giving her…a good/spiritual question to ask yourself is, how much of what you eat at lunch is how much YOU want to eat and how much Steph wants you to eat? Only you can answer this and grapple with it. My goal isn't to wage war between you and Steph—actually the opposite. No one wants a friend who functions as a parental watchdog but if your relationship has any of those nuances, that could potentially point to you needing to take more ownership over your own life so you're not being parented by others. Exploring these thoughts that are going on in your head is 100 percent SPIRITUAL—there is an underlying God-awareness involved here. In the end, what I'm getting at is that your own voice should be primary in fueling what you eat for lunch. (And, then, what you eat for lunch is a separate issue from the voice in your head telling you so. And please don't ask me what I ate for lunch today! All I can say is that I could've used something different but there was 100 percent satisfaction. :>) Make sense?

~work...when i slack at work i think of Charles Swindoll's book *improving your serve*...it makes me think of the times i have worked at younglife camps and worked that much harder b/c i know that i am doing it for God and for the kids...not for pay...i try and carry that over into my silly little job at the Spirit shop...

No doubt. I definitely hear you here. And this is going to be VERY difficult but I'd put this in the same ballpark with your Spanish class. I have trouble here too but with other things that seem to drain my freakin' soul in the doing of them. God is consistent, faithful, and diligent. There are times (Spirit Shop and Spanish class) when we don't see immediate return on our investment (outside of pay) and we're forced to find out how much consistency, faithfulness, and diligence we truly have. Pushing for excellence in the mundane minutia of flippin'

Spanish class and Spirit Shop is every bit where it's at! Reference the guy in the parking garage at Starbucks named Eric Johnson who is my current hero...the dude LOVES life and what does he do? It seems his primary job is to validate parking coupons inside the parking garage. So check this, he sucks carbon monoxide inside the parking garage all day and hands people cards to get validated once they get inside Chili's Too or Starbucks—I don't know where he comes up with the zeal for doing his job but he seems to love it. I think he's Superman.

~during many of my days i make a stop at CG...and chat with pals...common grounds is kind of a getaway...reminds me of the *cheers* theme song "where everybody knows your name, and they're always glad you came"...haha...

Same here. I'm there right now. At this second, I'm drinking a 2 percent Hazelnut Cream Cowboy. UNFLIPPIN' BELIEVABLE. The smell when you walk in the door, the taste, meeting new people, dialogue, laughter. But also this too—yesterday I was in here and had conversation with a UBCer—as soon as he took off, I began thinking about what a prideful idiot I was in one particular part of the conversation. I realized that the real intent of what I was telling him was full of self-promotion...rooted in lack of security/identity/not feeling satisfied enough in God's acceptance, etc...so my immediate next few minutes were spent verbally trashing myself. Then, this is ridiculous but perhaps realistic? I realized that the verbal trashing going on in my head wasn't an entirely healthy thing either. But there is something healthy, I believe, in having a level of disgust for places where pride surfaces. So in my thought space, I went back to sitting for a couple of minutes with what it means to AGAIN be accepted by God, what that acceptance entails... after thirty-two years, I still can't get this crap down!

~then comes dinner...same scenario as lunch..."therefore honor God w/ your body." i try!

(Same dialogue from above)

~there is always a time that i sit at my computer and waste time by reading online journals...this is super fun...and i make my entries mostly silly, i think i do it for attention really...ha... simply fun

Cool. I read three to five online journals as well every day and am close to starting a blog. In fact, I read recently that the average person checks ten blogs a day.

Then, seriously, I would explore the "attention" stuff you referenced here and look into that a bit deeper. At this point I'm probably shooting your wheels off with so much introspection, but it seems to me that there's something fairly destructive about some blogs that are out there these days. This is a whole other conversation. It can be a platform for passive-aggressive behavior; it has the potential to promote self-absorption (journals finding an audience); and, it also has the potential to stunt the growth of relationships, taking the place of times when the hard work of relationship-building needs to happen (face-to-face conversation, etc.).

Here's an idea: what if your blog was purposeful/headed somewhere. For example, what if your blog entries began taking on a different feel—what if you just began blogging about some of the minutia of your day (experiences, conversations, feelings, struggles with Spanish, etc.) from a God-awareness perspective. Again, this doesn't have to be blatant "spiritual talk"—I actually think that would frustrate some of your readers because it could turn too preachy (like me). But if you just detailed some of the things in your day with a sense of appreciation... heck, go into intimate detail about the particular taste of a hazelnut cowboy—ingredients, barista who served it, etc. I'm getting stupid here, but maybe you see what I'm getting at?

~steph and i normally have a "debriefing" time after class or at the end of the day...this is always fun and i think this is how we

keep our friendship going b/c we know it gets rocky sometimes...
~Meg and i do the same kind of thing...i love that girl!

Outstanding!

10
CHAPTER
THE ESSENCE OF CONVERSATION

I'm sitting here on a padded bench at a table in the back room of a local coffee shop feeling heavily weighted with apprehension about this specific chapter. On most days, this particular drink helps me begin my day on the right foot. It typically gathers my heart, lungs, ribs, and whatever else it finds in there and creates a sense of feng shui. However, even after enjoying half of my drink this morning, my innards are still in disarray. Even my favorite drink can't resolve my anxiety ...

I'm now at a place of putting into language those *particular* moments of deep connection with God. Deep connection with God likened to those between, say, a husband and wife. And yet this is no husband-wife relationship. Far more. Not so much sexual, but at times intimate. Thorough. Hidden. Transparent. Near.

How do you put into words moments of deep connection held between a husband and wife that are not always intended for others? And if those moments are then taken and placed on the market of public exchange, do they not lose their essence and sanctity in the transmission of those ideas? Here lies my anxiety. Does the husband or wife not, then, feel some sense of betrayal when their experience has gone public? So how do I talk about this primal, deep connection with God without betraying the essence of what it is? I have to admit the possibility that I may miss this entirely. In putting this thing into words, I may lose the sanctity of what it is.

I believe this is the reason Phyllis Tickle described prayer as "*a place*." "Prayer is a spot where we go just as surely as a church sanctuary is a place," she continues. "When we [pray], we are going into a place built from words. Or at least it's a place where words are the parameters, the walls into which we enter."[1] This place is not necessarily physical. It's not something that can be stripped, reduced, and formulated into a seven-step process. Still, the need is certainly there to find descriptive language to instruct others in its way.

In previous chapters, my aim has been to step back and erase the parameters that have existed for so long around what we call prayer. Clearly, I have no interest in a life of sporadic piety. I have no interest in creating a segmented kind of prayer that can be vocalized, then inventoried. For this reason, one could be amused by the fact that I've just now—in chapter 10—turned to describing that specific, isolated strand of minutes where intentional communication with God takes place. My goal has been to anchor our reality in a world thoroughly infused with God's presence—where the point of prayer is to facilitate an ongoing experience of God.

For the ancient Pharisees, prayer was always an end in itself where verbosity, quantity, volume, and duration measured levels of spirituality. However, I envision prayer differently. I imagine prayer to be standing, pointing, redirecting its own misplaced focus toward a transformative, seamless, whole-life interaction with God.

In recent chapters, my goal has been to pull us onto the same page by embracing a single, central definition of prayer—"any raising of the heart to God"—that is big enough to cover the full scope of life. Now that we are on the same page, I want to talk about that particular "raising of the heart to God" that is a deliberate, isolated event that happens in our mornings, afternoons, or evenings—that encounter between ourselves and God that takes place between 7:12 and 7:19 a.m., from 2:24 to 2:38 p.m., or from 11:42 p.m. to 2:18 a.m.

GOING INTO TO GET OUT OF

When Walter Brueggemann was in the sixth grade, a two-engine plane crashed in a cornfield near his house. He sprinted with his friends toward the crash to watch as the ambulance crew, with rubber gloves, lifted bloody pieces of the passengers from the crater the wreckage had carved in the cornfield. Brueggemann describes watching as they stuffed what they could find of those people into plastic bags. "But the most vivid memory that lingers in his mind was that of watching a 'woman standing next to him holding a baby, eating an apple.' He remembers wondering, 'How can she do that, now, here?' Only later did he understand, it was because 'she had no shame. She had no sense of incongruity, no sense of disproportion.' She was numb."[2]

At first reading, I didn't know what to do with this. A story so weighted. Initially, I wanted to inventory it. Categorize it. "Whoaaa. Heavy story."

There. Now I can shelve it. Place it in a file labeled "heavy stories" among the rest I've heard over the past five or six years or as far back as my memory takes me. But Brueggemann's experience wouldn't let me. It kept floating to the surface while I'd lie in bed or as I stared stupefied behind the wheel at intersections. After a couple of weeks it had infected my system, and it took as long to figure out why. It seems as though it had provided the diagnosis of the human way—or at least, *my* human way:

Numb. To stand, visibly watching so much disaster amidst wreckage without a trace of feeling.

Wreckage, that is—me. Inside and out.

I understand this. I understand what it feels like to experience indifference toward the person I've become, where (despite lengthy amounts of time spent in church) traits like self-promotion, dishonesty, and displacement rule the roost while perseverance, trust, and forgiveness are rarities. I understand what it's like to feel anesthetized and unresponsive to my friends, my family, God, and myself—for indifference to have taken over. I know what it's like for emotions and response to feel as though they've been muted. And experientially I feel as though I know the way out. To prayer I point, because prayer was meant to awaken. Even though, for some, prayer does the exact opposite of that for which it was created. That is, it doesn't stimulate one who is fully present and fully alive to God. For some, it simply encourages even greater levels of self-obsession. It resembles nothing more than an amplified diary where the current mood of the day has been plugged into a couple of speakers.

Well, it's Tuesday, and I'm sitting here at my desk trying to return some calls. I've been sooooooo unproductive lately. My procrastination is taking its toll. Oh yeah, I can't believe Trey said those things about Julie! Surely, he knew they'd get back to her, didn't he? And the busted radiator in my car won't be fixed until Friday. How am I going to get around between now and then? Oh well, I'll figure something out. Amen.

But if that's the essence of prayer, why include God? Why call it prayer? To be sure, prayer does not rotate around the self. It is not a monologue but a dialogue of intimate, heightened sensitivity and receptivity to God's presence, input, and perspective.

I guess it would help, for the sake of clarity, to first identify why God would want to connect with us in the first place. Why would God make Himself known to us on a personal level? Would it not be to speak truthfully to us about ourselves and the world in which we live—for our own good and the good of the world? That is, there is a transformative dimension to conversation with God and a missional one as well. A transformative dimension to prayer in which God affects change *in* us, and a missional dimension to prayer in which God affects change *through* us. No doubt, at times transformative prayer takes the shape of simple wordless enjoyment of the Divine, yet we still leave changed.

If you've ever found yourself in a position of saying, "God has never spoken to me," then you might ask yourself, "Why *should* God speak to me? What am I doing in life that would make speaking to me a reasonable thing for Him to do? Are we in business together in life? Or am I in business just for myself, trying to use 'a little God' to advance my projects?"[3]

Pulling us out of ourselves, prayer should stimulate transformation. However, I've found my instincts regarding prayer to be counterintuitive. The reverse of what I assume to be the path that will take me there. For example, most of us will agree that one who strives to follow Christ should exhibit a life marked by compassion, kindness, gentleness, joy, patience, self-control, and humility. Easy enough.

In order to exhibit humility, my natural instincts would say to walk with your head down, sink in your shoulders, and defer every compliment onto someone else.

Done.

To exhibit kindness, wear a constant smile from ear to ear, slightly tilt your head in conversation, and fulfill the quota of ten compliments per conversation.

Check.

If this is the model, many could experience spiritual transformation overnight! They'd wake up the next morning, employ a few mannerisms, and instantly "become Christlike," having gone from fully depraved to fully divine within twenty-four hours.

As we've discussed in previous chapters, authentic spirituality has nothing to do with acting (*upokriseus*). Radical change happens from the *inside out*. The primary learning here is not about how to act,

> ... just as the primary wrongness or problem is not what we do. Often what human beings do is so horrible that we can be excused, perhaps, for thinking that all that matters is stopping it. But this is an evasion of the real horror: the heart from which the terrible actions come. In both cases, it is *who we are* in our thoughts, feelings, dispositions, and choices—in the inner life—that counts. Profound transformation there is the only thing that can definitively conquer outward evil.[4]

We're a people prone to getting the cart out in front of the horse. We love shortcuts because, frankly, it's much easier to act compassionate, to act humble, and to act kind than for true compassion, humility, and kindness to be the actual condition of our hearts. A good way to think of spiritual transformation is "when our caved-in-on self energy is turned inside-out so that we're meaningfully and consistently abandoned to God."[5] Prayer that is transformative—not self-consumed—must, then, be aimed at turning our *insides out*. Not adorning the outer shell.

In Matthew 23:26, Jesus says, "First clean the inside of the cup and dish, and then the outside also will be clean." With the goal of inner change, many of us will be forced to relearn how to talk to God from where we're at, not where we should be. Those of us well-versed in church-speak will have difficulty relearning this first step because we've been trained in the ways of the external. Our first step is always to posture. To say what *should be* said. Even though, hilariously, another human being may not be in earshot within a fifty-yard radius.

In deeper levels of awareness, you begin to recognize how surface your actions actually are. That your outburst at work, for instance, was actually the final step in the assembly line of your own thoughts, dispositions, feelings, and choices—not the first or only step. So if prayer is going to function as a vehicle for radical change, we know its aim will be to leave the kiddy pool where surface actions are toyed with. It will, instead, create greater levels of self-awareness in the deep end where thoughts, intentions, and feelings take shape.

Jesus provides clear direction for these moments we set aside for deliberate communication with God. He instructs, "Here's what I want you to do: Find a quiet, secluded place so you won't be tempted to role-play before God. Just be there *as simply and honestly as you can manage*. The focus will shift from you to God, and you will begin to sense his grace" (Matt. 6:6, MSG, emphasis mine).

The question, then, is how might we find deeper levels of honesty so that our prayers ignite transformation in the interior aspects of our lives? Anne Lamott, writing about a different topic but most applicable nonetheless, says, "The problem is acceptance, which is something we're taught not to do. We're taught to improve uncomfortable situations, to change things, alleviate unpleasant feelings. But if you accept the reality that you have been given ... you free yourself to begin filling up again."[6] It's a perspective that I think Walter Brueggemann would echo as well. Until reading Brueggemann, I never considered such levels of honesty as "an act of bold faith"—rather, the opposite. But I certainly do now. When he writes about the gut-wrenchingly honest prayers we find in the Psalms, he says,

> It is an act of bold faith on the one hand, because it insists that the world must be experienced as it really is and not in some pretended way. On the other hand, it is bold because it insists that all such experiences of disorder are a proper subject for discourse with God. There is nothing out of bounds, nothing precluded or inappropriate. Everything properly belongs in this conversation of the heart. To withhold parts of life from that conversation is in fact to withhold part of life from the sovereignty of God. Thus these psalms make the important connection: everything must be *brought to speech*, and everything brought to speech must be *addressed to God*, who is the final reference for all of life.[7]

If we are to live in close proximity to Jesus, how can we open ourselves up to His presence in the hidden, remote areas? As the apostle Paul said, how might we "take captive every thought to make it obedient to Christ" (2 Cor. 10:5)?

Recently, I had a few rare minutes alone at the house, a sacred space in the absence of sound where the three-ring circus (my kids) is usually center stage. I sat down at the end of a table in the kitchen that looks out into the backyard, and I began praying. No more than two minutes into prayer, I had trailed off, replaying a scenario in my head from a couple of days prior when

I was driving through Minivan Row, the parking lot of a nearby church where Mother's Day Out was being held.

I'm driving in the lane closest to the church looking for a space in order to drop my daughter off when I notice a minivan driving about the same pace also looking for a parking space in the next lane over. We're both trekking down this parking lot on separate aisles but going the same direction at the same pace, and we come upon some open spaces on the end. I opened up my turn and began pulling into the last space when a woman—we'll call her "Satan's Helper"—not only turned into her spot *but continued* pulling on through into the parking space I was *clearly* turning into! I couldn't believe my eyes! I'm *a few feet* away from pulling into this parking space, and Satan's Helper is looking squarely at me, now from about five yards away, with a *smile* on her face! Instead of sticking her car in reverse and backing up into the previous spot, she shifts into park, turns off the car, and gets out to walk her kid inside. I'm now audibly addressing my windshield, "NO YOU DIDN'T!"

Luckily, my Passat is equipped with a front-end loader and a bumper forged with solid steel that allows me to ram things. Over and over, I hammered her minivan without any repercussion to my own vehicle. It was beautiful. One hundred percent satisfaction guaranteed ... or at least that's what I'm envisioning in the anger fantasy I've now trailed off into for the past six minutes sitting there in my kitchen. I'm panting for breath like I've just finished a marathon—all worked-up inside—although I haven't moved an inch.

In the past, I've been taught this is an utter failure in prayer. According to the prayer warriors, trailing off like this for several minutes just gave me an F for the day. But I now realize that my reality is centered here. This is not a random daydreaming episode. This is who I am. I am the sort of person who at times would love nothing more than to crush opposing vehicles in monster-truck fashion.

In sharp contrast to my former prayer life, I now become more aware of the world taking place in my hidden, interior life. Rather than dismissing this anger episode as "an obstacle to real prayer," I listen to the rhythm of my soul. Its hard, rapid, pulsating beat. If my mind keeps going back to these things, then maybe I have some issues that need tending to—issues around forgiveness, anger, or significance. Rather than dismissing these thoughts, I open myself up to God's presence and sit with them for a few minutes. And through a combination of prayer, meditation, Scripture reading, and silence, I become compassionate toward the person I was justifiably angry with.

In this case, it's Matthew 6:12 taken into every living organ within me. "Keep us forgiven with you and forgiving others" (MSG). Or as a more familiar translation reads, "And forgive us our debts, as we also have forgiven our debtors" (NAS). In this verse, we see a connection between our ability to forgive others and experiencing forgiveness from God on a deeply personal level ourselves.

So, first, I strive to live up close and personal with my own sinfulness. I become thoroughly aware of my own messed-up thoughts, motivations, and behaviors—the wreck I truly am. As long as I am aware of my own corrupt state, God's grace toward me remains constant. But when I push my sense of sinfulness further away, my relationships and approach to life become fragile because I've begun to live out of my own illusory sense of righteousness.

Then, I am (theoretically) able to extend forgiveness out of the very forgiveness from which God extends to me. When I am wronged, I (theoretically) am then able to extend forgiveness from level ground, not from a position of superiority. (Sadly, many people have come to believe that forgiveness means a number of things it does not. That, for instance, forgiveness is excusing, giving an individual permission for a behavior to be repeated. Others believe that forgiving means rescuing an individual from the consequences of his or her actions. Furthermore, many believe in the cliché "forgive and forget," and in the process they become boundary-less doormats for their family, friends, and coworkers.)

Surely, forgiveness is the act of setting free—them *and* us. We must recognize who is being hurt by our non-forgiveness. Do *they* burn with anger? Does *their* stomach remain knotted up for hours on end? Do *they* continually cycle and recycle the events of wrong-doing in their mind? Do *they* stay awake in the wee hours of night rehearsing what could be said or done for retribution? No, the pain is all ours.

FINISHED PRODUCT PRAYERS

When your prayer life pushes beyond meaningless ritual, trite clichés, and theatrical performance, lying on the other side is simple conversation. And I mean that in the truest sense of the word—"conversation."

Several months ago, one of the girls in our church began emailing me after experiencing frustration in her relationship with God, or at least what was left of her relationship with God. Much of her frustration was rooted in a number of negative circumstances that had gone on in her life over the past couple of years. At one point in our conversations, I recommended she read Brian McLaren's *Finding Faith*. She wisely accused me of "throwing a book at her," and all I could do was absorb the blame. I took the heat but insisted it might be a good resource, even though the title seems to suggest the intended audience lives outside of the church. I encouraged the book, not because she was coming from a place outside of the church but because she'd spent her entire life inside the church and still had questions that had been overlooked or dismissed as "lacking faith." Unlike the psalmist, she didn't feel the freedom to communicate openly and honestly about every aspect of her faith life. And this lack of honesty, I felt, was crippling her relationship with God.

In placing this description of conversational prayer within the context of a real-life relationship and actual conversation, it's my hope that the essence of prayer carries on, that it hasn't been stripped down to the bare essentials and dissected like a lab rat. I'd rather not manufacture a few lines of a fake prayer to provide an example of "prayer as conversation." Instead, I'd like to provide a real-life context where, hopefully, the sanctity of prayer is not lost.

For our purposes, we'll jump midstream into the email dialogue to the heart of my conversation with Faith.

----- Original Message -----
Sent: Sunday, January 02, 2005 8:11 PM
Subject: Re: Finding Faith

Hey Faith,

Thanks for jotting your thoughts.

About prayer...I just think that at the heart of prayer is the desire to have conversation with God (and emphasis on the word "conversation"). I do think we have the freedom to make our own choices. And obviously, I have gotten to a place where I truly think that prayer can affect the natural course of events. And uh oh, this could be raising alllll sorts of further questions. So be it. But I also think that you've addressed another big thing that happens in prayer which is a partial giving up of control. I say "partial" because I don't think God intended for us not to take ownership over our lives and not to be striving after the very things we are praying for. In fact, what if we said it was a *total* giving up of control in the final outcome of events but a *full* taking of responsibility in our part of the process?

Anyway, this could break out into a longer dialogue so I'll stop here for the time being and see what else you're thinking.

Kyle

Sent: Monday, January 03, 2005 12:34 PM
Subject: Re: Finding Faith

Kyle

That all makes sense and sounds wonderful—but how do I apply that to my life? Oh and please don't say "take a leap of Faith!"

I had always been comfortable with the idea of predestination and the way it basically renders prayer useless, because, that way, it was all on me, as far as my life and things that happened or didn't happen. I have always felt as though prayer is a way of setting God up, in that if things didn't turn out how you wanted, or how you asked Him to have them turn out, then that leaves room and gives reason to blame and doubt Him. I've always been more comfortable with taking responsibility for myself, therefore being the only one who's accountable in the end.

How does one get to that point where prayer is conversational? Where I am right now, prayer always feels forced, slightly staged, but more like I'm talking to myself. It feels very unnatural to me.

I'm going to have to get that down before I can address the issue of whether or not prayer holds any weight in which way the world spins. I don't mean to imply that God can't handle the things that I would put on Him—I'm just not comfortable with the part of actually asking for help. Because like I said, I feel like my faith would be under the weight of the outcomes and (right now especially) my faith doesn't need any more negative input.

Anyway, thanks for humoring me on this!

----- Original Message -----
Sent: Tuesday, January 04, 2005 10:57 AM
Subject: Re: Finding Faith

Hi Faith,

I think the conversational part begins by saying these very things that you said before. It's you verbally processing the thoughts that are in your head. See if this makes sense...I think we typically understand prayer to be voicing our "final product" thoughts, understandings, desires. But conversational prayer would be backing up a step and not just communicating to God our decisions, verdicts, and final ideas, but even the thoughts that are still in the works. So in your situation, but really, in MOST people's situations, it would be saying:

"God, (cut and paste your words) where I am right now prayer always feels forced, slightly staged, but more like I'm talking to myself. It feels very unnatural to me.

I'm going to have to get this thing down before I can address the issue of whether or not prayer holds any weight in which way the world spins. God, I don't mean to imply that You can't handle the things that I put on You—I'm just not comfortable with the part of actually asking for help. What's going on in me that makes that so difficult?

Like I said, God, with all that's gone in the past year, I feel like my faith would be under the weight of the outcomes and (right now especially) my faith doesn't need any more negative input...Amen."

Does that make any sense whatsoever?

Kyle

Sent: Tuesday, January 04, 2005 11:06 AM
Subject: Re: Finding Faith

Kyle,

So you meant "conversational" in the most literal sense of the word! That I can probably handle...

----- Original Message -----
Sent: Tuesday, January 04, 2005 11:22 AM
Subject: Re: Finding Faith

YES!!!

CONVERSATION OR SALES?

I felt his eyes on me as soon as the sole of my shoe hit the pavement. I didn't even have time to close my car door before the slick salesman was standing five yards away seeking common ground, "You like your Volkswagen?" *I knew this was a bad idea*, I thought to myself. *Is it too late to get back in and car shop online?*

"Yeah, I've loved it. It's been a great car."

"Jim Haskill," he said as he initiated with extended hand. "Kyle Lake." But somehow, even the handshake said it all. Stereotypical car salesman. All about control. His hand came swooping down from a foot higher than mine to greet me. Firm shake but subtly pulling mine in his direction.

It was Jim's lucky day. I was there precisely to test-drive a used vehicle I'd been researching online for a few weeks and was at a point where no amount of information could substitute sitting behind the wheel and experiencing the vehicle on the road for myself.

The test drive had to be Jim's forte. A few blocks down the road we hit a light, and he said, "Go ahead, punch it, feel the acceleration ... See? ... It's powerful. Great torque."

He, then, instructed me to take a left into a shopping center and park the car so he could show me a few things. I got out and began realizing how perfect this was. We're a couple of miles from the dealership, so I feel a little more relaxed. He popped the hood. We walked around to the front, and he began rattling off specs while pointing to various parts of the engine. "It's got a two-hundred-horsepower V6 with four valves per cylinder ... *blah, blah, blah*." Descriptive phrases—well rehearsed, but each description packed with a punch. As ignorant as I am, he could've been pointing to the tires while saying, "Notice the dual exhaust pipes and the keyless entry system"—and I would've said, "Oh, nice, nice."

Fifteen minutes later, I was back at the dealership sitting in a comfortable chair across from Jim with a cold Dr Pepper in hand. Across from Jim's desk were two customer chairs, and I noticed Jim's choice of seating immediately communicated a message. I was in one, and he was in the other—friendly, on *my* side. And within this casual atmosphere, we began negotiating. But not as I expected.

He didn't immediately begin talking numbers. He began running smack with smooth fluidity—questions cloaked in apparent concern as if he wanted to get to know me. After responding to questions about my job, how long I've lived in town, etc., he went into questions about who this vehicle was for—me, my wife, my family? The importance of good gas mileage on a scale from one to ten? There, at face value, were all the makings of a comfortable family atmosphere in which to do business ... comfortable seating, a free cold drink, and a salesman kicked back next to me—not across from me behind a desk—with his legs crossed, creating casual dialogue about a multi-thousand dollar expenditure as if we were talking about Aunt June's apple cobbler. The questions slid from his mouth as if they were second nature. That is, until he began to notice my responses didn't follow the smooth flow of this conversation he'd created.

Slipping just beneath his concerned, "Will this be the primary car your kids travel in or is there another?" was the question, "How much do your monthly payments need to be?" I was almost played once by a salesman who asked this question. I made the mistake of actually divulging my own budget needs, not realizing that in the process I had lost my buying power. "About $300," I said. And he responded, "$300 ... *up to what*?" "Oh, say, $350." Only later did I do the math in my head and realize that $50 a month is HUGE!" Never again would I respond to the question, "How much do your monthly payments need to be?" So this time, I lied. That makes two of us. "We've not quite figured that out yet."

Then Jim slipped another question into conversation before we'd ever begun actually negotiating the price of the car. "Will you be trading in a vehicle?" This one, I've learned. The answer is "No." If he knows up-front that a trade-in is involved, he can keep the selling price high. At the end of the day, it just *looks* like you've made a good deal once Jim pulls out a sheet of paper and subtracts the sticker price from the trade-in value. In reality, the buyer got conned twice. The new car stayed high while the trade-in price stayed low.

At one point during the negotiations of a high-priced purchase plan, Jim acted as if a thought suddenly popped into his head. "You know, there *might be* another way to get the monthly payments down … have you ever considered leasing? Then, in three years you can just turn your old car back in and take advantage of all the latest technological innovations!" But I'm fully aware of the advantages and disadvantages of leasing.

The further I got into conversation with Jim, the more I began to realize that, despite appearances, this was *not* conversation. Jim knew full well where he, I mean *we*, were headed. True conversation is marked by qualities you'll rarely find in a used car lot. There, you'll find well-rehearsed lines, manipulation, and a road map for where "conversation" should turn at every fork in the road. "You have a trade-in?" "What do you want your monthly payments to be?" "Have you considered leasing?" A response for every question. A premanufactured ploy designed to get exactly what you want.

The essence of conversation, though, is altogether different. It means you step into a dialogue not entirely knowing how the conversation will end or where the road will take you. It involves thoughts and feelings that are present in the moment. Intrinsic to true conversation are qualities like silence, listening, truthfulness, and presence. There are no generated responses designed to *sound* spiritual. If so, we may ask ourselves, who or what are we selling to God? Cars?

11 CHAPTER

SUPERNATURAL PHENOMENA

You can't possibly step into the world of the Scriptures and leave thinking God to be drab, dead, and silent. While there, you may very well encounter deaf and unresponsive humans. But a silent God? No. The number of experiences throughout Scripture would be too numerous for which to account: Jesus' baptism, Paul's experience on the Damascus road, the story of Ruth, Mary's angelic visit, Moses' multiple encounters, the prophets ... the list goes on and on. Some of these encounters with God are as real and casual as conversation with an old friend while other encounters border on the insane. In fact, we have many accounts of these God encounters in the ancient world that can't be evidenced by scientific laws of existence—though that doesn't mean they didn't happen. (The vast majority of humankind would agree that a number of things exist in today's world that can't readily be proven under a microscope—one example being love.)

The biblical accounts of the supernatural that I am referring to are dreams, visions, and angelic visitations, but I wouldn't say these examples are confined to the ancient world, either. Many of us have experienced for ourselves or at least heard of a real-life experience from a friend that defies natural law.

Krista and Michael Branch describe a terrifying but extraordinary experience shortly after watching *The Passion of the Christ* in the theater in 2004.

> We got up this morning like any other Sunday morning. We scurried around the house getting Kalon and Kassidy fed, and Krista went up to get Kenna. When she brought her downstairs, we saw that she was messy from a runny nose, and so I suggested to Krista that she give Kenna a shower. Krista took her in the bathroom and put her in the bathtub. We usually unscrew the stopper from the tub and all three kids play in the shower together. In the hurriedness of getting ready we neglected to unscrew the stopper and just pulled it out instead. What Krista didn't see was that Kenna had sat on the stopper and pushed it down so that the tub was slowly filling with water.[1]

Michael's wife, Krista, begins telling what happened next:

> Our computer was acting up and not accessing the website we were looking for, so I stayed for a little bit to try and figure out what the problem was. And of course I was listening to Kenna Beth the whole time ... periodically I would go back and make sure she was still playing, make sure she wasn't ready to get out. I was out of the bathroom for perhaps four minutes. Then I went to the bathroom door and saw water. Immediately my heart sank, and I thought, "Oh, no!" I ran to

> the shower and yanked the curtain back and saw her floating face down. I was certain she was dead. I started panicking ... She was gray . . she didn't have any color at all. Not purple, not blue. Just gray.[2]

The ambulance was called, and the paramedics came and sped Kenna Beth to a nearby schoolyard where a helicopter was waiting to airlift her to the closest hospital. Michael, then, describes what began happening as his daughter was flown to the hospital:

> I began to have visions—as Krista did—of the flogging scene (from the movie *The Passion of the Christ*) so vividly in my mind. The Scripture "by His stripes we are healed" continued to run through my mind ... "the chastisement of our peace was upon Him" ... I kept having visions of Jesus holding our baby and bringing her back to us.[3]

At this point, Michael and Krista felt a strong sense that Kenna would be okay, that she would live. Sure enough, Kenna began breathing again while the paramedics tried resuscitation. However, upon arriving at the hospital, the paramedics now feared that she would be left with severe brain damage. In the case of a drowning victim, brain damage will usually occur after four to six minutes. It is estimated Kenna Beth was without oxygen for a minimum of eight to ten minutes. Soon thereafter, doctors performed a CT scan but found no effects of brain damage whatsoever.

The Branches' experience is extraordinary! It is one of many accounts of supernatural phenomena taking place throughout the world today. Yet their story will certainly generate a number of different responses. Some, unconvinced by the time parameters provided, will chalk up the results to paramedic training and say, "This very situation is what paramedics are *trained* to do. They fully brought her to life as they had been certified to do, minimizing the possibility of brain damage along the way." And to be truthful, many of us have probably heard about or encountered "supernatural" events that could be explained quite rationally. There are many people today who are quick on the trigger to slap the label "SUPERNATURAL" on events that can be explained through applying only a few seconds of reason. But the Branches' experience doesn't seem to fit that bill. Others will say that, due to Michael and Krista's *special favor* with God, Kenna's life was miraculously saved. They may even begin worshiping the experience rather than the Source and feel a level of inferiority that they have never encountered anything so spectacular in their own lives.

Though there continues to be great debate as to whether the miraculous continues to take place today, Scripture provides no indication that miraculous experiences or supernatural modes of communication would cease with the ancient world or with the close of the scriptural canon. God is perfectly capable and continues to enact miraculous events and communicate via the supernatural today. I fully believe God continues to communicate with us through the medium of dreams, visions, and angelic visitations. However, the story of Aaron, Miriam, and Moses provides a window into God's end goal, His truest intentions.

In the twelfth chapter of the book of Numbers, Aaron and Miriam, absorbed in their own jealousy that God would speak to Moses and not them, were fuming.

> Miriam and Aaron talked against Moses behind his back because of his Cushite wife (he had married a Cushite woman). They said, "Is it only through Moses that God speaks? Doesn't he also speak through us?" God overheard their talk. Now the man Moses was a quietly humble man, more so than anyone living on Earth.

> God broke in suddenly on Moses and Aaron and Miriam saying, "Come out, you three, to the Tent of Meeting." The three went out. God descended in a Pillar of Cloud and stood at the entrance to the Tent. He called Aaron and Miriam to him. When they stepped out, he said, "Listen carefully to what I'm telling you. If there is a prophet of God among you, I make myself known to him in visions, I speak to him in dreams. But I don't do it that way with my servant Moses; he has the run of my entire house; I speak to him intimately, in person, in plain talk without riddles: He ponders the very form of God. So why did you show no reverence or respect in speaking against my servant, against Moses?" The anger of God blazed out against them. And then he left. (Num. 12:1-9, MSG)

Aaron and Miriam's jealous response proved they were incapable of being the sort of people with whom God could freely interact—as He did with Moses. Moses, characterized by humility, couldn't have cared less who had the inside track on "hearing God." For Moses, the ability to hear God wasn't prized as being especially important in the eyes of God. And the passage certainly seems to indicate that, from God's perspective, a distinction was made between His speaking in visions or dreams and His speaking "intimately, in person, in plain talk without riddles."

It becomes clear from the story that, though supernatural modes of communication were evident, they weren't *the ideal* form of communication between God and the individual. In fact, the story even tells why: God's ultimate desire isn't to create a relationship based on occasional, periodic experiences of ambiguity—dreams and visions. His ultimate desire is to create an ongoing relationship of conversation. For this reason, I don't believe these mediums—dreams, visions, angelic visitations, and other supernatural forms—should be sought after. "When the spectacular is *sought*, it is because of childishness in the personality. Children love the spectacular and show themselves as children by actively seeking it out."[4]

In 1 Corinthians 13, Paul reinforces this perspective by shifting the spotlight onto the sort of lifestyle for which we should be striving. In this chapter, the supernatural elements are downplayed in comparison to a continuous lifestyle of love.

> If I speak God's Word with power, revealing all his mysteries and making everything plain as day, and if I have faith that says to a mountain, "Jump," and it jumps, but I don't love, I'm nothing. If I give everything I own to the poor and even go to the stake to be burned as a martyr, but I don't love, I've gotten nowhere. So, no matter what I say, what I believe, and what I do, I'm bankrupt without love ... Inspired speech will be over some day; praying in tongues will end; understanding will reach its limit ... But for right now, until that completeness, we have three things to do to lead us toward that consummation: Trust steadily in God, hope unswervingly, love extravagantly. And the best of the three is love. (1 Cor. 13: 2-3, 8, 13, MSG)

E. Stanley Jones positions this perspective on miracles and the supernatural within the lifelong journey toward spiritual transformation. Jones says, "I believe in miracle, but not too much miracle, for too much miracle would weaken us, make us dependent on miracle instead of our obedience to natural law. Just enough miracle to let us know He is there, but not too much, lest we depend on it when we should depend on our own initiative and on his orderly processes for our development."[5]

Jones goes on to explain why a prayer life based on supernatural occurrences is not indicative of spiritual maturity.

> God cannot guide you in any way that is not Christ-like. Jesus was supreme sanity. There was nothing psychopathic about Him. He went off into no visions, no dreams. He got His guidance through prayer as you and I do. That is, He got His guidance when in control of His faculties, and not when out of control as in dreams. I do not say that God may not guide through a vision or dream; but if He does, it will be very seldom, and it will be because He cannot get hold of our normal processes to guide them. For God is found most clearly and beneficially in the normal rather than in the abnormal. And Jesus is the Normal, for He is the Norm.[6]

What we are doing here is creating an understanding of prayer that's been founded in full view of the sort of people God would have us be. As intentional followers of Christ, we have placed our lives on a specific trajectory. Prayer, then, should certainly propel us along that path. It would make no sense to create an understanding of "hearing God" that would not also push us toward becoming mature, whole-life learners of Christ. While I fully believe dreams, visions, and angelic visitations continue to take place all around us and may at times take place within us, I don't believe a life of prayer that *strives after* such things is indicative of greater depths of spiritual maturity, but less.

This is especially true in the case of decisions involving long-term commitment. It is tragic that someone could base a lifelong decision, such as a marriage partner or vocation, on supernatural phenomena rather than the full, informed use of their God-given faculties. A decision with as much weight and commitment should not be left to obscurities.

One final note: If we are always pushing toward more maturity in the way we relate to God, we now realize it will not be marked by seeking after repeated supernatural events. However, that doesn't mean we should become shut off to the possibility of the supernatural. I'm fairly certain the goal of the Christian is not to develop a life with God that looks remarkably similar to those six feet under.

12

CHAPTER

HEARING GOD OR SIMPLY SCHIZOPHRENIC?

It always amazes me how fluid and flippant some people interject mid-stream into conversation, "... so the other day God told me to (paint my car purple, have seven kids, begin a butterfly collection, start a band, marry my cousin) ..." Do they not notice I've now leaned in within five inches and have begun inspecting pupil dilation? Can't they hear my nose has shifted into a sniffing K-9 unit that readily detects Jim Beam or that my finger has just hit speed dial number six?

"DePaul Center for Mental Health"

(whispering) "Hey, it's Kyle."

"Oh, hey, Kyle. It's Sandy again. Just leave your cell phone on. We'll trace your location and send a couple of guys over to pick them up. How many?"

(whispering) "Just one. He's wearing tan chinos and a navy turtleneck. Send the guys on over and get him outta here. Quick. He hasn't begun seeing Gabriel or Raphael or Beelzebub, but give him another fifteen minutes, and he'll be there."

I want to ask, "Does even an ounce of hesitation surface before those words have been formed into the sentence, 'God told me to ...'? When was this filter removed? For the love! And, for the sake of Christianity's future, please turn the filter back on!"

GOD SPEAKING IN US

If you set aside the effects of the six-pack and the barbiturates, and also subtract the more spectacular divine encounters as not being God's normal daily mode of communication, you then shift your focus toward understanding the most frequent form of individual divine guidance found in the Scriptures. It's what has been referred to as "the still small voice." Keep in mind, though, that the end goal here will not resemble "the message-a-minute view." According to this view, the Christian's highest goal is to be found in the sort of relationship where God is sending you messages every minute of every day. The kind of relationship where you are constantly directed as to where you should go, what you should eat, with whom you should dialogue, and what you should say once there—every step of every day.

As I explained in chapter 3, the problem here is twofold: 1) this sort of dictatorial relationship would not encourage but *impede* our natural developmental process where we are striving to become more mature, responsible learners of Christ; and 2) the nature of our relationship with God is not mechanical or robotic. Rather, it functions very much as a father or mother relates to his or her child.

But let me be clear. While I don't believe God desires to create a tyrannical, micromanaging kind of relationship with us, I also don't mean to insinuate that God is mute. Just a few steps to the left, and we'll have created a lifeless figurine that sits on the bedside table. If God is truly that unresponsive, we might as well be praying to little Chewbacca standing there.

The most frequent form of divine interaction found in the Scriptures has been referred to as "the inner voice" and is most popularly described in 1 Kings 19. For our purposes, though, two different modes of God communication should be distinguished: 1) God's voice speaking *in* us about ourselves and the world around us; and 2) God's voice speaking *through* us to other human beings.

In the first, God communicates to us through our own thoughts and feelings that we have about ourselves and the people and happenings around us. In the second, God communicates through us and with us about the world and relationships surrounding us. Initially, let's look at the first ...

In 1 Kings 19, Elijah, a man of God, was on the move, running from a death threat. He made his way through the desert to a mountain called Horeb, and this happened:

> Then the word of God came to him: "So Elijah, what are you doing here?" "I've been working my heart out for the God-of-the-Angel-Armies," said Elijah. "The people of Israel have abandoned your covenant, destroyed the places of worship, and murdered your prophets. I'm the only one left, and now they're trying to kill me." Then he was told, "Go, stand on the mountain at attention before God. God will pass by." A hurricane wind ripped through the mountains and shattered the rocks before God, but God wasn't to be found in the wind; after the wind an earthquake, but God wasn't in the earthquake; and after the earthquake fire, but

> God wasn't in the fire; and after the fire a gentle and quiet whisper. (1 Kings 19:9-11, MSG)

Many translations read "a still small voice," and it's worded here as "a gentle and quiet whisper." The question is, how does "the still small voice" actually work? How does it actually function in daily life? How can we best describe the nuts and bolts of something so experiential?

The very second I hit that last question mark, I noticed that I used the phrase "nuts and bolts" to frame how I'd like to further explain "a gentle and quiet whisper." So, let's take a trip to Home Depot so we can disassemble this thing. All we'll need is a clamp, a twenty-six-piece screwdriver set, a wrench, and a couple of hex keys.

Our task would be much simpler if this thing was mechanical in nature, but it's not. Still, that doesn't mean we shouldn't try to understand the "still small voice" intelligibly. It doesn't mean we should abandon reason, the Scriptures, the history of the church, and our experience in arriving at a deeper sense of awareness and knowledge here. The very fact that it has been described as "gentle," "still," and "quiet" communicates volumes. Take, for instance, the descriptive word "small." The dictionary describes "small" as "being below the average in size or magnitude" or "lacking force or volume."[1]

In other words, the impression we're given does not indicate that the voice is not speaking but that the voice may not always be heard. It is not defined by volume, force, size, or magnitude. It does not impose itself or force its way into the forefront of our minds. So the issue is not its existence but our awareness. For this reason, it is possible for someone who constantly interacts with God in their thought space to not even be aware that the voice of God is something special.

Many times we have had the experience of feeling as though God was speaking directly to us through some particular medium. We say things like "That sermon today was specifically for me!" Or "That was exactly what I needed to hear!" We hear a song, and a few particular lines take flight like arrows and penetrate our hearts. We have conversation with a friend whose words bring such clarity to the predicament we're in, and we walk away changed, liberated, and lighter. In each of these cases, God communicates to us through a particular medium—most often, the words and actions of other human individuals found in a song, a sermon, a conversation, a novel, a movie.

When God speaks to us through "a gentle and quiet whisper," He is not using the medium of song, sermon, or something else external. Our own thought processes function as the medium. In normal day-to-day relationship, God uses our own thought processes even though we are in full control of our faculties—not out of control. We've not been hooked up to a machine or placed into a hypnotic state while hearing or sensing God's "gentle and quiet whisper."

There are biblical accounts of those who encountered an audible voice (Abraham as he sacrificed Isaac, Samuel as a child, those at the baptism of Jesus, and Saul on the road to Damascus), but that is not the voice I am referring to. Though it is a voice, I would still consider an "audible voice" to be supernatural in nature because it is not embodied by a particular person. I've never actually met anyone who has experienced the audible voice of God, at least not anyone sane.

What about content? What kinds of things will God say? When considering the content of this "gentle and quiet whisper," one of the questions we are answering is perhaps the second most popular question raised by those trying to follow God—right behind "What is God's will for my life?" The question we are answering is "How do I discern God's voice from the voice that is in my head?" Strangely enough, I believe the two are intrinsically tied. Let me explain.

The frequent mode of communication between God and us involves freely cognizant human beings who live in a cooperative relationship with God. This relationship doesn't function mechanically in the way that I operate my toaster oven. It doesn't involve dictation as in the message-a-minute view ... go here, go there, say this, say that. The content of this "gentle and quiet whisper" will typically not manipulate us like puppets on a string. Sure, there are numerous (and often authentic) stories about those who've sensed a distinct voice telling them to go to a particular school or to speak to a particular person, but these occasions don't make up the more frequent, day-to-day interaction we have with God. Reason? Because (as explained in chapter 3) minute-by-minute direction doesn't encourage the normal, healthy growth of an individual. Most often, the need for moment-by-moment authoritative command over where we should go and what we should say is but an indication of how little we are truly living with Him.

In the book of Acts, we don't find record of Paul being instructed by God as to the placement of every single step. Luke describes Paul's missionary journey in Acts 20 like this:

> With things back to normal, Paul called the disciples together and encouraged them to keep up the good work in Ephesus. Then, saying his good-byes, he left for Macedonia. Traveling through the country, passing from one gathering to another, he gave constant encouragement, lifting their spirits and charging them with fresh hope. Then he came to Greece and stayed on for three months. Just as he was about to sail for Syria, the Jews cooked up a plot against him. So he went the other

> way, by land back through Macedonia, and gave them the slip. They went on ahead and waited for us in Troas. Meanwhile, we stayed in Philippi for Passover Week, and then set sail. Within five days we were again in Troas and stayed a week. We met on Sunday to worship and celebrate the Master's Supper. Paul addressed the congregation. Our plan was to leave first thing in the morning, but Paul talked on, way past midnight. (Acts 20:1-3, 5-7, MSG)

The impression we're given here is not of Paul being commanded by God as to which city he should pursue and what he should say once he was there—though that doesn't rule out God's involvement (chapter 8)! In fact, verse 4 describes a situation in which Paul altered his missionary travel plans on the fly as he was faced with hostile threats. All to say, the content of "the still small voice" *may* include direction—go here, go there, do this, do that—but, most often, that will not be the case.

A more common aspect of "the gentle and quiet whisper" involves our own thoughts and accompanied feelings about ourselves, those around us, and the events of daily life. Proverbs 20:27 says, "The spirit of man is the lamp of the Lord, searching all the innermost parts of his being" (NAS). As we grow deeper in maturity, we become aware of the train on which our thoughts and feelings usually travel. God takes our self-awareness—the way we relate to our family, friends, and God; our attitudes toward possessions, sexuality, and health; our fears; our preoccupation with reputation and appearance—and He marks those thoughts and feelings with His presence and direction. It is as if God is taking a lamp into the remote areas of our inner world and directing our eyes to things deserving attention—attitudes, fears, insecurities, preoccupations. He then sheds light on those areas and makes known the truth about those very things—His perspective and desires.

Unfortunately, we can never know with certainty which is the voice of God and which is our own. It is, by nature, *experiential.* Not an experience involving fireworks. No sirens will sound. It's not like we've been given a device like the one at the restaurant that buzzes when our table is ready. "Uhhhp, there it goes. That thought buzzed. It's God. He's saying ..."

Sure, we can narrow the playing field by eliminating thoughts that run contrary to Scripture, but even Scripture has been used to justify the most insane behaviors. It's not fail-safe. In examining our thoughts against the backdrop of Scripture, we'd have to be more precise in describing the type of scriptural use we're talking about. We'd have to eliminate proof-texting—the case that happens all too often where individuals strip passages out of their context to validate a decision that's already been set in concrete. Not only would we need to eliminate proof-texting, but we'd also need to beware of translating this sacred text as if it's an instruction manual for assembling a trampoline. Some passages immediately translate into the twenty-first century within seconds while many others require further understanding. The historical setting in which those passages come provides a world of difference, not only in our understanding of Scripture but especially the way Scripture strengthens the "still small voice."

> In 1 Corinthians 11, for example, we find women being advised not to have short hair and men being informed that on them long hair is shameful. Such things are clearly incidental. On more serious matters, in Mark 10, Jesus tells the truly fine young man who had come to him that he must sell all he has and give the proceeds to the poor. This too, contrary to what many have thought, is *incidental to people generally* (for Jesus did not ask this of everyone He met). In the particular case of this young man, of course, Jesus' directive went right

> to the heart of his special problem with wealth. But it is not a principle to which all must conform. Why? Because it is not a teaching emerging from the whole of Scripture; and it should not, without further consideration and guidance, be taken as God's word to you or anyone else.[2]

So someone may sound as though they are acting on "the word of God" and even come equipped with a verse and text to back it. The more discerning individuals, though, will not base direction or guidance on the "incidentals" from Scripture but the principles—centrally located in the life and actions of Jesus.

By way of content, there are additional ways we can narrow the search in discerning God's voice from our own. If we pay close attention to the life of Jesus and the lives of the disciples, we'll notice their journeys frequently entailed disappointment, conflict, failure, suffering, and little funds. A sweeping look at Matthew's Gospel account finds chapters 8, 10, 12, 13, 14, 16, 21, 22, 26, and 27 involving some level of conflict, failure, or suffering. So we can also be sure that God's voice will never promise us a life void of difficulty and suffering. Contrary to the popularity of the Health & Wealth Gospel, our lives aren't guaranteed financial success and prosperity. We're also not exempt from sickness and disease.

With these thoughts in mind, my approach to the inner voice goes like this: I am not preoccupied every second of every day trying to decipher which is the voice of God and which is the voice of Kyle. I am preoccupied with what it means to become a more faithful follower of Christ in every spectrum of life. I move confidently through the day, striving to approach people and events in ways I think Jesus would while maintaining an attentive awareness to the thoughts and feelings going on within me. The voice of God, then, becomes more familiar only as a byproduct of my pursuits, not as the end goal. I am not pursuing a voice. I am pursuing Christ.

GOD SPEAKING THROUGH US

While this isn't the primary subject of this book, let's briefly look at the second means of communication: God's voice speaking through us to another human being. In this case, God's thoughts and our thoughts aren't mutually exclusive. It involves God speaking to us *through* our own thought processes and *with* our own thought processes. In fact, there are times when it seems as though, *in the act of speaking*, our words are given a heightened degree of clarity—whereby both the listener AND ourselves are influenced. However, just because God has spoken through us does not also mean that, in the process, we laid aside our own intentions, desires, and knowledge.

Naturally, those who have been in the habit of living in the way of Christ will most often find themselves in this scenario—where their voice and God's voice work hand in hand. The longer they follow God, the more their desires and thought processes line up with God's.

The Bible provides the best example here. Consider what we have in Scripture. Real, live human beings—probably in dire need of a good odor-masking agent, a thorough shower, and a heavy dose of Dr. Scholl's foot spray—speaking and writing conjointly with God. The letter of Philippians, for example, holds the word of God and the words of Paul and Timothy hand in hand. The first verse even says, "Paul and Timothy, both of us committed servants of Christ Jesus, write this letter to all the Christians in Philippi, pastors and ministers included" (Phil. 1:1, MSG). Scripture did not come about through dictation. Every letter, every narrative, every song, every line of poetry in the Bible was authored, sung, or spoken by a particular person writing in a particular predicament with particular stories to tell and conflicts to navigate—by writers with full use of their faculties, not under hypnosis.

Notice, though, we must distinguish God's speaking to us via our own thought processes from *channeling*. Channeling is a pagan practice in which one is believed to have lost use of his faculties in order to freely function as a "spirit guide." Orthodox Christianity has never adopted channeling as a biblical practice, although some Christians talk about God's speaking in ways that sound strangely similar to channeling. If we have been instrumental in communicating a profound message to another person, we must not confuse our part in the process as being mechanical in nature as though God used us as we use an electric drill.

Pastors and priests strive to function in this way on Sunday mornings, but to ever think God is speaking *through* a pastor on a Sunday morning and not *with* the pastor is a mistaken elevation of the pastor and a violation of his or her humanness. At times, a pastor or speaker will sincerely and innocently pray, "God, help me to get out of the way so You can speak clearly." But to think he is simply channeling God is a naïve assumption and can potentially make for a destructive use of the platform. All pastors are fully human but not fully divine. There's only one Jesus.

For this reason and many more, "The Lord told me to tell you ..." is dangerous language to use. Many Christians reference God speaking through them as though they had no part in the matter—as if their own brains and desires weren't actually operating at the time. Even if there is 98 percent assurance that the voice I heard was "the voice of God," I've never found a substantial or healthy reason for attributing the "word" to God in public. No doubt, I've seen "The Lord told me to tell you ..." used as a power play on a number of occasions or for self-promotion or simple dishonesty, but I've never found a viable reason as to why an individual wouldn't take full responsibility for their "word from the Lord."

No matter what words fall from our lips, they are always ours. If they are ever refused, denied, or displaced, it is but an indication that we are not taking seriously enough our own personal journey of discipleship.

In instances where direction from God is sought on behalf of a friend, precaution should always be taken. Larry Crabb provides wise insight for when we find ourselves in the situation of praying for a friend.

> My version of prayer as battle is to imagine my friend in the presence of the Trinity and to eavesdrop on their conversation. I claim to hear neither audible voices or inerrant messages. I simply reflect on what I know of God as revealed in scripture—the Father's unconditional love, the Son's atoning grace, the Spirit's gentle rhythm—and I imagine what they are right now saying to my friend and what they are thinking and feeling about him.[3]

Since there is no claim to "audible voices" or "inerrant messages," what follows is not a loaded, high-pressured "*The Lord told me to tell you* ..." Instead, it is a suggestive "Have you considered ..." or, in the very least, "I feel as though ..."

Make no mistake. God's communication in us, through us, and with us will always encourage our lifelong journey of becoming mature followers of Christ. That interchange will not stunt our growth or make us childish in living and acting in the ways of Christ. He will always push us forward.

13

CHAPTER

DEAR GARTH

My friend and theologian Garth Brooks said that "some of God's greatest gifts are unanswered prayers." But that was in 1990. *Well* before he pulled that Chris Gaines stunt. Sure, he lived the missional life with his friends in low places, but what kind of prayer was Chris Gaines? Answered or unanswered?

Garth, perhaps if you had taken the time to consult ME, I could've told you that your country-singer-turned-fictional-rock-star-to-attract-wider-audience ploy would prove to be a major miscalculation. But no. You had to haul off and experience it for yourself, didn't you? I would've also helped you reword that line, "that just because he doesn't answer doesn't mean he don't care." In the first place, Garth, you've not used proper grammar. This was the only thing that bugged me about that song as I tearfully sang along in the car. And secondly, I think you've misunderstood God's apparent silence. Hear me out: I don't believe God is mute. And since I believe that God fully intends to communicate His intentions with us, silence would be likened to the sort of passive-aggressive behavior found in many relationships today. You know, "passive-aggressive"—where an individual chooses to fight by disengaging from the argument or suddenly shifting his or her attention to something completely unrelated. Sadly, I've done this with my wife a number of times, and it's completely unfair. Garth, can I sleep at your place the next time I'm redirected to the couch? The couch can't sustain a full night's rest. Only Sunday afternoons.

It seems as though there are times when some play the "God is silent" card as a defense mechanism. Not you, Garth. I'm talking about *other* people. I can't make out from your song if you really think that God was silent during your high school years when you prayed about marrying your girlfriend, or if you're using the word "unanswered" as a lyrical literary technique. So which is it? When you said "unanswered," did you really mean "answered" (since it turned out to be a good thing that you didn't marry your high school sweetheart)? I'm just an idiot when it comes to literary techniques like this and songs with multiple levels of meaning. Musically, and most of the time, I operate on one level: surface. Heck, it takes me seven or eight listens before I even catch a song's lyrics in the first place! This has not proven to be advantageous as my little kids now speak Shizzle fluently. Or at least that's what I think it is. Jude, one of my twin two-year-old boys, got angry with me the other day and was popping off at the mouth, something about "gin and juice."

All right, Garth, here it is. It seems as though God could respond to our individual requests in a few different ways, but I've found that there are two mistaken interpretations that wreak havoc and can potentially destroy a person's relationship with God. So I want to explain these two interpretations to "answered/unanswered prayer" and why they can be so destructive. I realize that our shared human experience provides a lot of direction, but don't get your feelings hurt if I don't reference your song in my explanation, okay?

ANYTHING GOES

First, this is the most popular mistaken interpretation to "answered prayer." It's called "Anything Goes."You'll hear this philosophy embraced by way of the phrase *"I guess it just wasn't meant to be."* Meaning, whatever happens in life is also what God *wanted* to see happen—leaving no room for our part in the process and nullifying the possibility of any sort of interchange between God and us. Realistically, Garth, you play a substantial role in creating what *happens*. It's just that you and I don't control *all of the outcomes*. However, I'm not saying that whatever you do is also the will of God. (Again, Garth, I remind you of that Chris Gaines fiasco. Was that *really* the will of God for you to double as Chris Gaines? I think not.)

But I *am* saying that there is reason for prayer and there is reason for you and me getting off our bums and applying the physical form of belief to the very things for which we're praying. God had called Moses to free His people from slavery. In Exodus 32, God was incensed that His people would go back to making idols for worship.

> God spoke to Moses, "Go! Get down there! Your people whom you brought up from the land of Egypt have fallen to pieces. In no time at all they've turned away from the way I commanded them: They made a molten calf and worshiped it. They've sacrificed to it and said, 'These are the gods, O Israel, that brought you up from the land of Egypt!'" God said to Moses, "I look at this people—oh! what a stubborn, hard-headed people! Let me alone now, give my anger free reign to burst into flames and incinerate them. But I'll make a great nation out of you." Moses tried to calm his God down. He said, "Why, God, would you lose your temper with your people? Why, you brought them out of Egypt

> in a tremendous demonstration of power and strength. Why let the Egyptians say, 'He had it in for them—he brought them out so he could kill them in the mountains, wipe them right off the face of the Earth.' Stop your anger. Think twice about bringing evil against your people! Think of Abraham, Isaac, and Israel, your servants to whom you gave your word, telling them 'I will give you many children, as many as the stars in the sky, and I'll give this land to your children as their land forever.'" And God did think twice. He decided not to do the evil he had threatened against his people. (Exod. 32:7-14, MSG)

In other translations, verse 14 says that God "changed His mind" about the harm He was about to inflict. Good news for those of us who feel as though our prayers do hold weight with God! In Luke 11, Jesus even encourages us to pray with persistence for the things we desperately desire.

So after a prayer has been offered, the tragedy is to assume that all outcomes are the will of God. What we seem to forget is that humans play a vital role in the process as well. 1 Timothy 2:3-5 says, "This is the way our Savior God wants us to live. He wants not only us but everyone saved, you know, everyone to get to know the truth we've learned: that there's one God and only one, and one Priest-Mediator between God and us—Jesus" (MSG). Now, even though it is God's desire for "everyone to get to know the truth," that's not exactly what is happening, is it? Even though God's desire is for all of us to experience that sense of rescue and to live in the way of Christ, He doesn't overpower us to make that happen (though He, of course, has the ability to). Through prayer and human action, we play a part in the grand scheme of how things turn out in this universe! Just because a relationship, job, or financial investment turned out the way it did does not automatically mean the outcome was the will of God.

SILENCE OR "UNANSWERED PRAYERS"

The second mistaken interpretation to God's response is silence. The difficulty with putting an end to this "silence" perspective is that it requires a fairly thorough understanding and experience of the previous chapter on "the inner voice."

Basically, I contend that God is *not* unresponsive like the pagan idols of the ancient world. He *will* respond, though it may not be what we are looking for. A different, unanticipated response *is* a response (as opposed to silence). As the story we looked at earlier continues, we find another fascinating account of the conversation between God and Moses. This time, Moses was the frustrated one.

> Moses said to God, "Look, you tell me, 'Lead this people,' but you don't let me know whom you're going to send with me. You tell me, 'I know you well and you are special to me.' If I am so special to you, let me in on your plans. That way, I will continue being special to you. Don't forget, this is your people, your responsibility." God said, "My presence will go with you. I'll see the journey to the end." Moses said, "If your presence doesn't take the lead here, call this trip off right now. How else will it be known that you're with me in this, with me and your people? Are you traveling with us or not? How else will we know that we're special, I and your people, among all other people on this planet Earth?" God said to Moses: "All right. Just as you say; this also I will do, for I know you well and you are special to me. I know you by name." (Exod. 33:12-17, MSG)

What's fascinating is that Moses wanted in on God's plans, but God didn't respond like Moses wanted. God simply said, "My presence will go with you. I'll see the journey to the end." And that's exactly what God did. He continued providing Moses with His presence throughout their journeys, but initially the answer was not what Moses was looking for. Garth, this may be what you're talking about when you sing of "unanswered prayers." Technically speaking, though, that's not what it is. It's not silence. It is a clear response. It's just that this response requires trust, patience, and a strong level of attentiveness to that habitual inner conversation we share with God.

One of my favorite Garrison Keillor quotes illustrates this well. In *Lake Wobegon Days*, Keillor tells the story of a man who gets into his Buick in the middle of a blizzard even though he can barely see "across the yard to the barn, and his wife and child are pleading with him to please not go into town."[1] On the way in, he begins to realize how preposterous this trip actually is as he plows through snowdrifts for four miles on the way to the corner store. He runs in and buys a carton of Pall Malls. A mile south of town, the wind kicks up, and suddenly he can't see anything—the ditches, his hood ornament—so he drives slower and slower searching out "the slightest clues of road, until there is none—no sky, no horizon, only dazzling white."[2] So he opens his car door, leans out, and hangs from the steering wheel while looking for tire tracks with his face close to the ground. As the car slips off the road, he realizes that he's simiply following the track of his own left front tire into the deep ditch. The car sits deeply in the snow, the only way out is to slip through the car window. He's about a quarter-mile from home, and he realizes the cigarettes aren't in his car. They must be back at the corner store still sitting on the counter. Now, the trip appears to have been worthless. "Town was a long way to go in a blizzard for the pleasure of coming back home. He could have driven his car straight into the ditch and saved everyone the worry. But what a lucky man. Some luck lies in not getting what you thought you wanted but getting what you have, which once you have it you may be smart enough to see is what you would have wanted had you known."[3] He takes a deep breath and, more sensibly, begins the short walk to his house where his family loves him and will be glad to see his face.

In the same way, I think petitionary prayer will often set us on a particular journey in which we develop a heightened sensitivity to our truer needs. Toward the end of that particular journey, we may realize that what we discovered and how God responded was altogether different from the thing we were pursuing at the outset—perhaps we discovered a renewed sense of clarity, a new relationship, a change of direction, or a renewed love and appreciation for our immediate relationships. Again, though, these are all responses, not byproducts of a mute God.

All right, Garth, I'll let you go. I've taken up enough of your time. But I do have one last request. Now that you've read this chapter, would you reissue that 1990 *No Fences* album? I took the liberty of rewriting the chorus of those lyrics to "Unanswered Prayers" so they'd be more consistent with our conversation here. You may need to pick up the pace quite a bit while you're singing a couple of the lines to make it flow a little better.

> *Sometimes I thank God for ANSWERED prayers*
> *Remember when you're talking to the man upstairs*
> *That just because you can't make out exactly what's going on*
> *or what the still small voice is telling you doesn't mean He*
> *don't care or that He's an unresponsive pagan idol like the*
> *ones in Thessalonica*
> *Some of God's greatest gifts are ANSWERED prayers*

You can send my royalties to:
1701 Dutton Avenue
Waco, Texas 76706

Sincerely,
Kyle

14
CHAPTER
THE POINT

In the previous pages, I've tried to frame prayer with a wider lens, holding disdain for compartments and parameters, settling for nothing less than a life of truthfulness and transparency while offering our whole lives. Sure, we could promote the Pharisaical way by focusing our efforts on moments of sporadic piety. We could very well employ a few mannerisms—clinching the eyes tighter or stretching the arms wider. We could interject a couple of more clichés, regurgitating the words "blessing," "fellowship," "in the word," and "confess." We could even measure levels of spirituality by quantity, volume, and duration. We could. But why? Why settle for form when we could have substance?

If we want more from our lives with God, we could forge new territory. Terrain that's not readily covered. We could allow prayer to develop fully into what it's already becoming—the fluid, seamless, open-ended conversation with God that threads our day. Conversation that is truly con-versation. "Con" meaning "together" or "with," "verse" meaning "to familiarize by study or experience."[1] So experientially familiarizing ourselves with God. Not to God but with God. Becoming fully present with our unfinished, nonrehearsed thoughts and feelings and allowing God's presence and perspective there. Even amidst the most disjointed, awkward ramblings that lack melody or rhythm.

With Jesus leading the way, we've been instructed to address God on such intimate terms (Mark 14:36, Rom. 8:15), allowing God into the basement—which at times has even been off-limits to ourselves. There's something about this—the way Christians are encouraged to pray—that is peculiar to Christianity. It provides the very essence of prayer, and it's on this note that I want to end.

Every single religion that's ever existed has had some way of communicating with the supreme being it worships. Prayer is not something in which Christians alone participate. There is just something about the way we as Christians pray that is distinctive, that is peculiar to Christianity. Tony Jones describes this well.

> Ancient civilizations such as Greece and Rome abounded with gods, most of which had human attributes and appetites. Conversations between deities and humans went like this: Humans communicated with their gods by offering sacrifices to appease the gods' tempestuous wrath (and consequently avoid storms, war, pestilence, illness, fire, and hardships of every sort) and to earn good fortune (and consequently receive proper weather, bountiful harvests, good health, plenty of wealth, victory in battle, and blessings of every other kind). The gods communicated to human via augurs, Roman religious officials who read the future in the clouds, they'd track birds in flight, and trace the entrails of animals, and would then pronounce, "The gods are angry!" Or, "The gods are appeased!"[2]

That was how god-to-human communication was practiced at the time Jesus introduced the world to a different way of communication.

In a first-century Jewish temple, six trumpet-shaped money chests were placed specifically for the collection of alms—in order to attract the attention of others. If you drop two coins in the trumpet, that's not going to receive much notice. But everyone will notice when someone drops twenty coins into the trumpet. Especially if one of the temple officers were to blow a horn to signal the giving of a very large gift! So, what has now become the motivation to give alms? With this in mind, Jesus instructs His disciples saying,

> Be especially careful when you are trying to be good so that you don't make a performance out of it. It might be good theater, but the God who made you won't be applauding. When you do something for someone else, don't call attention to yourself. You've seen them in action, I'm sure—"playactors" I call them—treating prayer meeting and street corner alike as a stage, acting compassionate as long as someone is watching, playing to the crowds. They get applause, true, but that's all they get. When you help someone out, don't think about how it looks. Just do it—quietly and unobtrusively. That is the way your God, who conceived you in love, working behind the scenes, helps you out. (Matt. 6:1-4, MSG)

According to Jewish doctrine, almsgiving provided a high return. So it must have been shocking for these people to hear Jesus say, "They get applause, true, but that's all they get." One author says that they were not giving but buying. They wanted the praise of men so they paid for it. And this sets the stage for what Jesus said about prayer.

> And when you come before God, don't turn that into a theatrical production either. All these people making a regular show out of their prayers, hoping for stardom! Do you think God sits in a box seat? Here's what I want you to do: Find a quiet, secluded place so you won't be tempted to role-play before God. Just be there as simply and honestly as you can manage. The focus will shift from you to God, and you will begin to sense his grace. (Matt. 6:5-6, MSG)

Jesus gives us a picture of people who took satisfaction in the length of their prayers. To be precise, His indictment wasn't that they prayed long prayers. Have you ever seen the length of Jesus' prayer in John 17? Now, that's a long prayer. Jesus' indictment was that they took great satisfaction in the length of their prayers—a crucial difference.

When I was a freshman in college, I met a girl who was also an incoming freshman whom I thought to be a younger version of Heidi Klum. Only problem was that I found out she had a boyfriend who also was a freshman. Initially, I thought this to be a minor obstacle, since I likened their relationship to the short-lived Julia Roberts/Lyle Lovett union. It just didn't make sense. The part I couldn't get around was the fact that the two of them had been dating for a couple of years, obviously a solid relationship. Hope was lost, and I moved on.

My junior year, two years later, they broke up—she freed herself from the shackles of that pipsqueak, and I had the boldness to do something that practically created a revival at Baylor University.

I asked her out.

You know, on "a date." Not the—if you happen to be at the same place I'm going to be at on Friday night, maybe, just maybe, we'll spend a few minutes text messaging each other from across the room. No, I'm talking about the—I'm going to drive to your apartment, get out of my car, walk up to the door, knock, escort you back to the car, go to dinner, and maybe dessert or coffee.

After two years, I had a date with this godsend, and my roommates were hyping me up for it. They were all giving me ideas on what I ought to do. One of my roommates was telling me, "You need to buy some flowers for her, pick up some carryout from Olive Garden, and head out to the lake. You can take a candle and a blanket and have a candlelit picnic under the stars." And I said, "Mike, I hardly know her. Don't you think the full-court press would be a little strong?"

Another roommate was steering me in the opposite direction. "You need to play hard to get ... make sure you see her earlier in the day on Saturday and then when you go out Saturday night, wear the same thing you had on earlier so she knows that you're not too eager for this date." And I said, "But I am ... maybe I ought to show her a little more than that?"

When Saturday night came, the anxiety level was out the roof. I remember thinking, "Wow, after *two* years, I finally have a date with this girl. I can't believe it!" Around 7:00 p.m., I started toward the front door of my apartment when I heard my roommates chanting my name. Somehow they had turned my name into a rhythmic, two-syllable shout with every ounce of testosterone in their bodies: "KY-LE ... KY-LE ... KY-LE ... KY-LE." By the time I was five yards from the door, they had set up a sort of soccer-mom post-game tunnel with their overarching arms interlocked, paving my way out the front door. With arms in the air, I pranced out the door as if I'd just scored the go-ahead goal at the World Cup.

Unfortunately, though, the date hit turbulence early on. I made my way to her apartment okay and even to her front door. But when walking her back to the car, things quickly went south. I politely opened the door of the car for her, but for some reason—maybe I was too eager or I wasn't thinking clearly—I didn't give her enough time to get her entire body inside the car before I shut the door. Idiot! We'd not gotten three minutes into the date, and she had a gash in her leg the length of pencil. And this was before we'd even made it to the restaurant.

Dinner didn't improve. Maybe I was trying too hard to recover, I don't know, but the conversation seemed to hit a brick wall at every turn. Then, to cap things off—and this was the best—toward the end of the date, I was driving her back to her apartment, and the band on the radio was an odd sort of mix between punk and rap. In a lame attempt at humor, I inserted an insensitive joke—something about the guy singing lead vocals sounding like he has Tourette's. Insensitive because she, then, proceeded to inform me that her younger brother has Tourette's. Unbelievable.

And that was the end of that.

A date I had looked forward to for *two* years could not have come to an end any sooner. I had hyped this date and joined in banter with my friends over this thing, such to the extent that the date had taken on a life of its own. In retrospect, there was *the girl* I was dying to take out ... and then there was *the date*. Somehow, over time, they became two very distinct things.

This seems to always be the danger with prayer and perhaps the essence of what Jesus communicated to the Pharisees in Matthew 6. "Religious leaders, your prayers have taken on a life of their own. Maybe at one time, there was a simple love for God.

And your communication with God facilitated that. But somewhere along the way, prayer became the point, not God. That is, *praying* became the point of prayer. Rather than God being the point of prayer."

Following in the way of Jesus, *praying* has never been the point of prayer. God has always been the point.

APPENDIX
HISTORICAL PRAYER

It is one of the more unique experiences to come across a prayer, written and verbalized by someone else, that perfectly articulates your very own thoughts and feelings, and then find out that prayer was voiced 1,478 years ago in a remote village off the coast of Italy. This is what historical prayer does. It connects us with the ongoing story of God that has been unfolding for thousands of years.

We live in a rapidly changing, fast-paced world that can leave us feeling as though we've been misplaced. Using ancient prayers as a tool to connect with God can often target our precise location—where we are in our spiritual journey. These prayers and practices bring a sense of rootedness when they're utilized. They remind us we are not alone, that the terrain we're covering has been walked before.

In the next couple of pages, I will offer some contemplative practices that could be utilized to liven prayer. These exercises have deeply historical roots, but there's no need to be intimidated by their terms. Learning Greek isn't needed to use them. Each practice will be briefly explained, and then several examples of ancient prayer will follow in chronological order. Allow these prayers and practices to travel space and time to become your own.

LECTIO DIVINA

The term *lectio divina* simply means "sacred reading" or "holy reading." It involves reading a passage of Scripture over and over in a spirit of contemplation. It seems the most difficult aspect of *lectio divina* is trying to prevent yourself from reading Scripture as though it were under a microscope. Take a short passage and repeat it several times slowly, aloud. Stay attentive to the thoughts and images that surface while you're reading the passage, allowing God to speak to you through the Scripture.

IGNATIAN CONTEMPLATION

Ignatian contemplation was used by Saint Ignatius of Loyola in the early part of the sixteenth century. There are several exercises associated with Ignatian contemplation. One is similar to *lectio divina*, but requires using your imagination to visualize the setting of a biblical text with you in it ... listening to the Sermon on the Mount, standing at the foot of the cross, visiting the house of Zaccheus. Another is called *examen*, and not only uses your imagination but also your memory. Take an event from your past and recall the event for a few moments as it actually happened. Then become open to the Spirit of God stepping into the event—prompting, influencing, and speaking to you.

DEEP BREATHING

We are interconnected people who cannot be divided piecemeal—a head that functions apart from the heart or thoughts that function apart from our emotions. We are whole. Deep-breathing exercises are intended to allow our physical bodies to affect our spiritual perspectives, rather than vice versa. This practice could be utilized every time you begin conversation with God. Breathe in slowly for a count of five, then breathe out slowly, counting the same amount. The intent is for your soul to be pulled out of its normal pace and find a different rhythm for listening to the interior voice of God.

A SAMPLING OF ANCIENT PRAYERS (IN CHRONOLOGICAL ORDER)

Clement of Rome, 30-100[1]

We beg you, Lord, to help and defend us. Deliver the oppressed, pity the insignificant, raise the fallen, show yourself to the needy, heal the sick, bring back those of your people who have gone astray, feed the hungry, lift up the weak, take off the prisoners' chains. May every nation come to know that you alone are God, that Jesus Christ is your child, that we are your people, the sheep of your pasture.[2]

Saint Clement of Alexandria, 153-217

O God, make us children of quietness, and heirs of peace.[3]

Gregory of Nazianzus, 325-389

O transcendent, almighty God,
What words can sing your praises?
No tongue can describe you.
No mind can probe your mystery.
Yet all speech springs from you,
And all thought stems from you.
All creation proclaims you,
All creatures revere you.
Every gust of wind breathes a prayer to you,
Every rustling tree sings a hymn to you.
All things are upheld by you.

And they move according to your harmonious design.
The whole world longs for you,
And all people desire you.
Yet you have set yourself apart,
You are far beyond our grasp.
You are the purpose of all that exists,
But you do not let us understand you.
Lord, I want to speak to you.
By what name shall I call you?[4]

Augustine of Hippo, 354-430

You are great, Lord, and greatly to be praised. Great is your power, and of your wisdom there is no end. And man, who is part of what you have created, desires to praise you. Yes, even though he carries his mortality wherever he goes, as the proof of his sin and testimony of your justice, man desires to praise you. For you have stirred up his heart so that he takes pleasure in praising you. You have created us for yourself, and our hearts are restless until they rest in you.[5]

Bernard of Clairvaux, 1090-1153

Jesus, how sweet is the very thought of you! You fill my heart with joy. The sweetness of your love surpasses the sweetness of honey. Nothing sweeter than you can be described; no words can express the joy of your love. Only those who have tasted your love for themselves can comprehend it. In your love you listen to all my prayers, even when my wishes are childish, my words confused, and my thoughts foolish. And you answer my prayers, not according to my own misdirected desires, which would bring only bitter misery, but according to my real needs, which brings me sweet joy. Thank you, Jesus, for giving yourself to me.[6]

Francis of Assisi, 1182-1226

Lord, make me an instrument of your peace.
Where there is hatred, let me sow love.
Where there is injury, let me sow pardon.
Where there is doubt, let me sow faith.
Where there is despair, let me give hope.
Where there is darkness, let me give light.
Where there is sadness, let me give joy.
O divine master, grant that I may
not try to be understood, but to understand;
not try to be loved, but to love.
Because it is in giving that we receive,
in forgiving that we are forgiven,
and in dying that we are born to eternal life.[7]

Julian of Norwich, c.1342-c.1413

God, of your goodness,
give me yourself
for you are enough for me.
And only in you
do I have everything.[8]

Catherine of Siena, 1347-1380

Eternal Father, you said, "Let us make humankind to our own image and likeness." Thus you were willing to share with us your own greatness. You gave us the intellect to share your truth. You gave us the wisdom to share your goodness. And you gave us the free will to love that which is true and just.

Why did you so dignify us? It was because you looked upon us, and fell in love with us. It was love which first prompted you to create us; and it was love which caused you to share with us your truth and goodness.

Yet your heart must break when you see us turn against you. You must weep when you see us abusing our intellect in pursuit of that which is false. You must cry with pain when we distort our wisdom in order to justify evil.

But you never desert us. Out of the same love that caused you to create us, you have now sent your only Son to save us. He is your perfect image and likeness, and so through him we can be restored to your image and likeness.[9]

Ignatius of Loyola, 1491-1556

Take, Lord, and receive all my freedom, my memory, my intelligence and my will—all that I have and possess. You, Lord, have given those things to me. I now give them back to you, Lord. All belongs to you. Dispose of those gifts according to your will. I ask only for your love and your grace, for they are enough for me.[10]

Teresa of Avila, 1515-1582

It is a comfort, Lord, to know that you did not entrust the fulfillment of your will to one so pitiable as me. I would have to be very good if the accomplishment of your will were in my hands. Although my will is still self-centered, I give it, Lord, freely to you.[11]

John of the Cross, 1542-1591

O living flame of love,
that wounds my soul so tenderly
in its deepest center;
Since by your grace
I can endure your touch,
perfect your work in me
according to your will.[12]

Brother Lawrence, c.1605-1691

My God, you are always close to me. In obedience to you, I must now apply myself to outward things. Yet, as I do, I pray that you will give me the grace of your presence. And to this end I ask that you will assist my work, receive its fruits as an offering to you, and all the while direct all my affections to you.[13]

Fenelon, 1651-1715

You know better than I how much I love you, Lord. You know it and I know it not, for nothing is more hidden from me than the depths of my own heart. I desire to love you; I fear that I do not love you enough. I beseech you to grant me the fullness of pure love. Behold my desire; you have given it to me. Behold in your creature what you have placed there. O God, you love me enough to inspire me to love you forever; behold not my sins. Behold your mercy and my love.[14]

Soren Kierkegaard, 1813-1855

Calm my troubled heart; give me peace. O Lord, calm the waves of this heart, calm its tempests! Calm thyself, O my soul, so that the divine can act in thee! Calm thyself, O my soul, so that God is able to repose in thee, so that his peace may cover thee! Yes, Father in heaven, often have we found that the world cannot give us peace, but makes us feel that thou art able to give peace; let us know the truth of thy promise: that the whole world may not be able to take away thy peace.[15]

NOTES

(RE)UNDERSTANDING PRAYER

Introduction

1. *www.imdb.com/title/tt0098258/quotes*, accessed July 25, 2005.
2. *www.imdb.com/title/tt0119229/quotes*, accessed July 25, 2005.
3. *www.imdb.com/title/tt0120601/quotes*, accessed July 25, 2005.
4. *www.imdb.com/title/tt0146882/quotes*, accessed July 25, 2005.
5. "A Shrink Gets Stretched," ChristianityToday.com, *www.christianity-today.com/ct/2003/005/7.52.html*, accessed January 4, 2005.

Chapter 3: The Message-a-Minute View

1. Dallas Willard, *Hearing God* (Downers Grove, IL: InterVarsity Press, 1984) p. 31.
2. Ibid.

Chapter 4: The Foxtrot

1. *www.dictionary.com*, accessed February 1, 2005.

Chapter 5: D-A-Double D-Y-M-A-C

1. J.B. Phillips, *Your God Is Too Small* (New York: Touchstone Books, 1997) p. 38.

2. "Falling Snow Can Create a Noisy Nuisance ... Underwater," ScienceDaily.com, *www.sciencedaily.com/releases/2000/03/000305122454.htm*, accessed April 5, 2005.
3. Anne Lamott, *Bird by Bird* (New York: Anchor Books, 1994) p. 22.

Chapter 6: Prayer as Drama

1. *members.tripod.com/~scriptsg_den/dumbanddumber.html*, accessed March 20, 2005.
2. John Jeremiah Sullivan, "Upon This Rock," Men.Style.com: The Online Home of Details and GQ, *www.men.style.com/gq/features/landing?id=content_301*, accessed March 25, 2005.
3. Ibid.
4. Ibid.
5. Ibid.
6. Ibid.
7. Brennan Manning. "Honestly Speaking," *Conversations Journal*, Spring 2003, p. 26.
8. *www.riehlworld.net/dave*, accessed March 25, 2005.
9. *www.dictionary.com*, accessed March 29, 2005.

Chapter 7: Recipe Theology

1. *www.dictionary.com*, accessed April 18, 2005.
2. "A Shrink Gets Stretched," ChristianityToday.com, *www.christianitytoday.com/ct/2003/005/7.52.html*, accessed April 19, 2005.
3. Ibid.
4. *www.bibletexts.com/sh/hg/h0539.htm*, accessed April 25, 2005.
5. Todd Hunter, "Rehearsing the Gospel of Jesus," Emergent Convention, San Diego, CA, 2003.
6. For the Gnostic, evil is the material or physical world. Salvation comes through the knowledge of the spirit world and denial of the material. The spirit world was an invisible world. Asceticism is essential for salvation, as one must renounce the physical body along with its lustful cravings if one would ever hope to obtain the greater spiritual illumination. The spirit man or essence is the real, while the physical

man is unreal and temporal. The Gnostic religion preaches a hidden wisdom or knowledge ("gnosis") only to a select group as necessary for salvation or escape from this world. However, the concept of body was celebrated by primitive Christians, and although Christianity was focused on the spirit as distinct from "the flesh," the experience was of an embodied and not disembodied spirit. This does not pose a problem if one has a worldview where spirit and body are not mutually exclusive. And this was certainly the case before philosophical dualism became the dominant philosophical paradigm in the West. The dualism of early Christianity was the spirit versus the flesh, not the spirit versus the body.

Chapter 8: The Eastern Way

1. Dallas Willard, *The Divine Conspiracy* (San Francisco: HarperCollins, 1998) p. 67.
2. Ibid.
3. Dallas Willard, *Hearing God* (InterVarsity Press, Downers Grove, IL: 1984) p. 75.
4. Rob Bell, "Exploring the Edges of Theology Without Freaking Out Your Flock," Emergent Convention, San Diego, CA, 2003.
5. F.L. Cross and E.A. Livingstone, eds. *The Oxford Dictionary of the Christian Church* (Oxford: Oxford, 1997) p. 1315.
6. Tony Jones, *Pray* (Th1nk Books, Colorado Springs, CO: 2003).
7. Brother Lawrence, *The Practice of the Presence of God* (New Kensington, PA: Whitaker House, 1982) p. 37-38.
8. Kathleen Norris, *The Cloister Walk* (New York: Riverhead Books, 1996) p. 280.
9. Ibid.
10. Ibid., p. 280-281.
11. Ibid., p. 281.
12. Ibid., p. 281.
13. Ibid., p. 281-282.
14. *www.goodgroundpress.com/index.asp?PageAction=Custom&ID=87*, accessed July 21, 2005.

Chapter 10: The Essence of Conversation

1. "The Shaping of a (Prayer) Life," VineyardUSA.org, *www.vineyardusa.org/publications/newsletters/cutting_edge/2002_winter/prayer_life.htm*, accessed February 5, 2005.

2. "Hear the Weeping," explorefaith.org, *www.explorefaith.org/LentenHomily04.11.03.html*, accessed May 5, 2004.

3. Dallas Willard, *Hearing God* (Downers Grove, IL: InterVarsity Press, 1984) p. 70.

4. Dallas Willard, *Renovation of the Heart* (Colorado Springs, CO: NavPress, 2002) p. 24.

5. Larry Crabb, "The Sure Route to Madness," *Conversations Journal*, Spring 2003, p. 10.

6. Anne Lamott, *Bird by Bird* (New York: Anchor Books, 1994) p. 178.

7. Walter Brueggemann, *The Message of the Psalms* (Minneapolis: Augsburg Press, 1984) p. 52.

Chapter 11: Supernatural Phenomena

1. Jody Eldred, *Changed Lives: Miracles of the Passion* (Eugene, OR: Harvest House, 2004) p. 50.

2. Ibid., p. 51.

3. Ibid., p. 53-54.

4. Dallas Willard, *Hearing God* (Downers Grove, IL: InterVarsity Press, 1984) p. 112.

5. E. Stanley Jones, *A Song of Ascents* (Nashville: Abingdon, 1979) p. 191.

6. E. Stanley Jones, *The Way* (Nashville: Abingdon/Cokesbury, 1946) p. 283.

Chapter 12: Hearing God or Simply Schizophrenic?

1. *www.dictionary.com*, accessed May 19, 2005.

2. Dallas Willard, *Hearing God* (Downers Grove, IL: InterVarsity Press, 1984) p. 179.

3. Larry Crabb, "Prayer Is Battle," *Conversations Journal*, Spring 2004, p. 26.

Chapter 13: Dear Garth

1. Garrison Keillor, *Lake Wobegon Days* (New York: Penguin Books, 1985) p. 336.
2. Ibid., p. 336-337.
3. Ibid., p. 337.

Chapter 14: The Point

1. *www.dictionary.com*, accessed July 21, 2005.
2. Tony Jones, *Pray* (Colorado Springs, CO: Th1nk Books, 2003) p. 17.

Appendix: Historical Prayer

1. *www.ccel.org* consulted for all dates.
2. Dorothy Stewart, *The Westminster Collection of Christian Prayers* (Louisville, KY: Westminster Knox Press, 2002) p. 346.
3. Angela Ashwin, *The Book of a Thousand Prayers* (Grand Rapids, MI: Zondervan, 1996) p. 201.
4. Robert van de Weyer, *The HarperCollins Book of Prayers* (Edison, NJ: Castle Books, 1997) p. 175.
5. Stewart, p. 282.
6. van de Weyer, p. 66.
7. *www.poetseers.org/spiritual_and_devotional_poets/christian/st__francis_of_asissi/poems/prayer_of_st__francis*, accessed April 10, 2005.
8. *www.exeter.anglican.org/showart.php?tn=newsminichrist&ai=50*, accessed April 10, 2005.
9. van de Weyer, p. 90.
10. *www.ewtn.com/library/mary/ignaitu2.htm*, accessed April 9, 2005.
11. Ashwin, p. 27.
12. Ashwin, p. 48.
13. Stewart, p. 373-374.
14. Ashwin, p. 49.
15. Ashwin, p. 98.

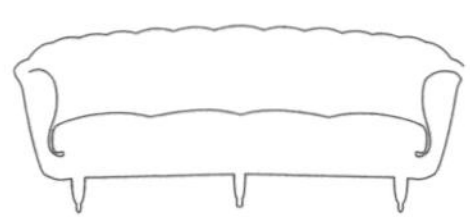